Study Guide and Exercise Workbook
for Muchinsky's
Psychology Applied to Work

Sixth Edition

Marc C. Marchese
King's College

Wadsworth
Thomson Learning™

Australia • Canada • Denmark • Japan • Mexico • New Zealand • Philippines
Puerto Rico • Singapore • South Africa • Spain • United Kingdom • United States

For permission to use material from this text, contact us by
> **Web:** www.thomsonrights.com
> **Fax:** 1-800-730-2215
> **Phone:** 1-800-730-2214

ISBN 0-534-36254-0

For more information, contact
Wadsworth/Thomson Learning
10 Davis Drive
Belmont, CA 94002-3098
USA
www.wadsworth.com

International Headquarters
Thomson Learning
290 Harbor Drive, 2nd Floor
Stamford, CT 06902-7477
USA

UK/Europe/Middle East
Thomson Learning
Berkshire House
168-173 High Holborn
London WC1V 7AA
United Kingdom

Asia
Thomson Learning
60 Albert Complex
Singapore 189969

Canada
Nelson/Thomson Learning
1120 Birchmount Road
Scarborough, Ontario M1K 5G4
Canada

Author Note

Marc C. Marchese received his Ph.D. in industrial/organizational psychology from Iowa State University in 1992. Currently, he is an assistant professor in the human resources management department at King's College in Wilkes-Barre, Pennsylvania. He has taught courses in personnel training and development, psychological testing, graduate and undergraduate introduction to HRM, organizational theory, employment and labor law, and organizational communication. His research interests include job enrichment, part-time/full-time employee differences, and personnel selection.

Preface

This study guide was designed to be used with Muchinsky's sixth edition of <u>Psychology Applied to Work</u>. For each chapter, the study guide begins with an outline of **key terms and concepts**. You could use the outline either to take notes when reading the text or you could use the outline to quiz yourself when preparing for exams. Next, the study guide has a listing of the relevant **web sites** for the text chapters. You could use these web sites as starting points for course assignments. Moreover, at the end of each chapter the study guide presents a variety of interesting exercises. The objective of these exercises is to help you apply and understand the material presented in class and in the textbook. Since the pages of the study guide are **perforated**, your instructor may ask you to bring the study guide to class, and hand in the exercises. Finally, to help you further prepare for exams five sample multiple-choice questions for each chapter are available to you at:

http://psychology.wadsworth.com/study_center/index.shtml

I hope you find this study guide valuable as you complete this course. Good luck!

Sincerely,

Marc C. Marchese, Ph.D.
Assistant Professor of HRM
King's College

TABLE OF CONTENTS

CHAPTER 6   TRAINING & DEVELOPMENT

CHAPTER 7   PERFORMANCE APPRAISAL

CHAPTER 8   ORGANIZATIONS & WORK TEAMS

CHAPTER 9   ORGANIZATIONAL ATTITUDES and BEHAVIOR

CHAPTER 10 STRESS and WELL-BEING AT WORK

Chapter 1: Study Guide

THE FOUNDATIONS OF I/O PSYCHOLOGY

The following is a list of key names, terms and concepts from Chapter 1. As a way to help you understand the chapter and get to know the material, go through each of the terms and describe them fully. Then compare your responses to the responses in the textbook.

Note that you should not rely solely on key term lists when studying for your class exams. Instead, you should go back and make sure you thoroughly understand the content of the chapters and the content of your class notes.

Psychology:

American Psychological Association (APA):

Industrial/Organizational Psychology:

a) Division 14 of the APA (What is Division 14 and who belongs?):

b) Percent of psychologists in the I/O area:

c) Two sides of I/O Psychology: Science versus practice (Do you understand how they differ?):

d) FOUR main work settings of I/O Psychologists (list them here):

Fields of I/O Psychology (Can you see how they are different?)**:**

   a) Selection and Placement:

   b) Training and Development:

   c) Performance Management:

   d) Organization Development:

   e) Quality of Worklife:

   f) Ergonomics:

Licensing and Certification of Psychologists:

    a) licensing law:

    b) certification law:

    c) purpose of licensing and certification:

    d) controversy regarding licensure of I/O Psychologists (What is it?):

The Early Years of I/O Psychology (1900-1916) Write general notes here, then summarize the main contributions of each of the following individuals.

a) W.L. Bryan:

b) Frank and Lillian Gilbreth:

c) Walter Dill Scott:

d) Frederick W. Taylor:

e) Hugo Munsterberg:

World War I (1917-1918) Write general notes about this time period's significance to I/O psychology here, identify the names and terms associated with this era:

    a) Robert Yerkes:

    b) Army Alpha:

    c) Army Beta:

    d) <u>Journal of Applied Psychology</u>:

Between the Wars (1919-1940):

   a) Psychological Corporation:

   b) James Cattell:

   c) Hawthorne studies:

   d) Hawthorne effect (draw and describe):

World War II (1941-1945):

    a) Army General Classification Test (AGCT):

    b) situational stress tests:

Governmental Intervention (1964-present):

    a) Title VII of the Civil Rights Act of 1964:

b) Americans with Disabilities Act of 1990:

c) Civil Rights Act of 1991:

d) Project A:

Cross-Cultural I/O Psychology:

FOUR Significant changes in world conditions which affect our worklives:

1)

2)

3)

4)

The Mandate of I/O Psychology:

Web Sites for Chapter 1

Here are some general I/O psychology and human resources web sites that may be beneficial to you throughout this course.

1) http://www.siop.org/

   This is the SIOP web site.

2) http://www.albany.edu/~kjw11/hr.html

   This is the web site of the HR division of the Academy of Management.

3) http://www.aom.pace.edu/

   This is the web site of the Academy of Management.

4) http://www.nbs.ntu.ac.uk/staff/lyerj/hrm_link.htm

   This web site that has categories for various HR and I/O psychology topics.

5) http://www.siop.org/TIP/TIP.html

   This web site has TIP (The Industrial Psychologist) on-line.

6) http://www.shrm.org

   This is the web site for the Society of Human Resources Management.

Exercise 1-1: Applying I/O Psychology to Your Last Job

The first chapter of your textbook introduced you to the field and history of I/O Psychology. If someone asked you what an I/O psychologist does, could you answer him or her now? If not, you should review the chapter once again. Also realize your ideas of what an I/O psychologist does will become more concrete and better defined as you continue through your I/O psychology course.

As described in the book, an I/O psychologist may be concerned with a wide variety of organizational issues. Following are some of the things an I/O psychologist might do:

* write job descriptions so that employees and managers are clear about job responsibilities

* develop and improve performance appraisal forms to assess how workers are doing on the job

* develop training programs to help workers learn and improve on the job

* study whether or not current training programs are effective or whether they need to be improved

* develop selection tests to help managers select the best qualified individual for a position

* conduct job satisfaction surveys to see if workers are satisfied with their jobs

* conduct research to understand problems of turnover, absenteeism, and motivation

* design methods to improve communication between workers and management

* improve work environments for workers

* improve productivity by job redesign

* attempt to reduce work stress among employees

* design workshops to help individuals cope with retirement issues

This exercise will make you think about how I/O psychology might be used in the last job you held (or are working at right now). Then, as you continue learning about I/O psychology, you can keep the example of the last job you held (or the job you are working at right now) in your mind. If you have never held a job, please ask a roommate, friend, or family member to help you complete this exercise.

1.   Describe the most recent job that you have held (or a job you are working at currently). What types of duties did your job entail?

2.   What might an I/O psychologist do in the organization that you worked for? List at least five things. For example, if you were not trained very well when you started your job, you might suggest that an I/O psychologist come in and evaluate how workers were trained. Please be very specific and give some explanation.

Exercise 1-2: SIOP and Student Membership

Becoming a student affiliate of the Society for Industrial and Organizational Psychology (SIOP)

It may be of interest to a small number of you taking this industrial/organizational psychology course to pursue knowledge in this field further. You may, for example, want to become a student affiliate of SIOP. Recall from your textbook that "SIOP" is Division 14 of APA and is also known as the Society for Industrial/Organizational Psychology. While professional members of SIOP are required to also belong to APA or APS, student members can join SIOP without belonging to APA or APS. An individual applying for student affiliate status in SIOP does not need to be majoring in psychology, but must have a faculty member sign to verify that he or she is a student in good standing and is engaged in study related to I/O psychology.

As a student member of SIOP, you will receive a subscription to The Industrial-Organizational Psychologist (known as "TIP"). This publication will give you information about job opportunities in I/O Psychology (usually for Ph.D.-level applicants), recent legal issues relevant to the workplace, SIOP's annual conference held in the spring of each year, and other information that professionals in the I/O field need. Because TIP is written for professionals in the I/O field, you may only be interested in its content if your career goal is to work in this area.

Student membership in SIOP is only $10.00. In order to be accepted into SIOP as a student member, you need to submit the following information to SIOP Headquarters:

Date:
Name:
Mailing Address:
Educational Background:
     Name and Address of Institution:
     Degree you are pursuing:
     Year you expect your degree:
Advisor's Name:
Advisor's Signature:

Send your application along with a check for $10.00 to:
SIOP Headquarters
745 Haskins Road, Suite A
P.O. Box 87
Bowling Green, OH 43402-0087

The telephone number for SIOP, should you have any questions, is 419-353-0032. The fax number is 419-352-2645.

Becoming a student member of the Society for Human Resource Management
          Another national organization students might find appealing is known as the Society for Human Resource Management, or SHRM. SHRM is a much larger organization than SIOP, and includes individuals with a background in human resources. You are eligible for student membership if (1) you are enrolled in at least six semester hours (or eight quarter hours) per term and (2) if your planned or completed coursework supports a demonstrated interest in human resource management. You do not have to be planning on graduate school to benefit from this organization.
          Student members of SHRM receive several benefits, including a monthly magazine (HRMagazine) and newsletter (HRNews). HRMagazine includes in-depth articles on several applied human resource management issues, such as performance appraisal, training, compensation, and sexual harassment. HRNews is a great resource for job openings in human resources and legal updates on human resource issues. Student membership in SHRM may be more appropriate than TIP (described previously) for students who want to work in human resources without an M.S. or Ph.D. In general, SHRM publications tend to be more applied in nature than SIOP publications.
          Student membership in SHRM is $35.00 (as of 1996). Because SHRM is a large national organization, there may be a local chapter of SHRM near you that has regular meetings. Your university may even have a student chapter with a faculty adviser. For more information about joining SHRM, call or write:

          Society for Human Resource Management
          606 N. Washington Street
          Alexandria, VA 22314-1997
          Phone: 703-548-3440
          Student program office phone: 1-800-283-SHRM
          World Wide Web Site: http://www.shrm.org

Exercise 1-3: Graduate School in I/O Psychology

Your textbook will introduce you to the exciting field of Industrial/Organizational (I/O) Psychology. The concepts you learn in this class (e.g., about job analysis, selection, performance appraisal, training workers, motivating workers, job satisfaction, job design, stress in the workplace, unions, etc.) will be a tremendous help to you professionally *no matter what your major or career interest.* Most students who take industrial/ organizational psychology as a class, in fact, are not planning to practice I/O Psychology but will use the concepts they learn in the course in their own respective fields.

Nevertheless, some of you may be interested in pursuing I/O Psychology as a career specialty. For those individuals, this exercise will lead you through the steps for finding out more information about graduate school opportunities in the field. As discussed in the book, a graduate education (M.S. or Ph.D.) is necessary to practice as an I/O Psychologist. It should be noted, however, that some individuals are able to find jobs in a human resources department with a B.S. or B.A. degree in psychology and a strong emphasis in industrial psychology or business.

Graduate school is not for everyone! Admission into graduate programs is competitive, admitting only students that have a high grade point average, good GRE scores (an admission test you must take to get into most graduate programs in psychology), research experience, and strong letters of recommendation. Masters programs typically take two years, including summers. Ph.D. programs typically take students between four and six years to complete. Students should really like to read and study, and at the Ph.D. level, they should be willing to take several statistics courses and do multiple research projects. Although M.S. programs tend to be more application-oriented and Ph.D. programs tend to be more research-oriented, both types of programs usually follow a research/practitioner model where both science and practice are emphasized.

If you are interested in learning more about applying for graduate school in I/O Psychology, this exercise will be very helpful for you. Read and complete the following steps. I also strongly encourage you to discuss your interests with a faculty member. Discussing your interests with a faculty member will help you determine whether or not graduate school is appropriate for you.

Steps to Complete

1. Take at least one course in I/O Psychology to make sure the field interests you. Ask your instructor questions about career opportunities in I/O Psychology. As discussed in the book, there are opportunities in industry, consulting, government, and academia. Career options differ depending on whether you earn an M.S. or Ph.D. What career options in I/O appeal to you? Write them here.

2. Meet with faculty members to discuss what classes you should be taking to best prepare yourself for graduate work in I/O Psychology. It is helpful for individuals who want a Ph.D. in I/O Psychology to have a strong quantitative and science background. It is also helpful, although not necessary, for individuals to have taken several I/O or business-related courses. List all quantitative (math, statistics, computer, or research methods), science, I/O, and business-related courses you have taken:

    Quantitative:

    Science:

    Business-related:

3.   Faculty members typically advise their students to apply for at least five different graduate programs. You will thus need to know where there are graduate programs available in I/O Psychology. There are two books that may help you with this information:

a. Graduate Study in Psychology (1994 with 1995 Addendum) published by the American Psychological Association (APA). This book offers information about graduate programs in all areas of psychology. It will tell you about location of programs and admission requirements. Your library or psychology department probably has a copy of this book you can check out. Otherwise, you can order it for approximately $20 by calling 1-800-374-2721 (APA).

b. Graduate Training Programs in Industrial/Organizational Psychology (1992; a new version will be out in mid-1996), published by the Society for Industrial/Organizational Psychology (SIOP). This book offers specific information about graduate programs in I/O Psychology. You can order it by writing to the SIOP Administrative Office, P.O. Box 87, Bowling Green, OH 43402-0087 (Phone: 419-353-0032). This book is about $5.00.

Request information from all prospective schools to which you might apply. Ideally, this should be done about one year before you hope to attend graduate school. Simply send a postcard to each I/O program you are interested in and ask them to send you information about their program and admission standards. List the programs that interest you or that you wrote to for information here:

4. Most graduate programs require that you take the GRE. Your scores on the GRE will be interpreted as a measure of your general intellectual ability along with your grade point average. There are books available at most book stores that will help you to prepare for the GRE. It is recommended that you take the GRE during October of the year before the academic year you want to start graduate school. There is usually an academic assistance center or placement center at most universities where you can get information about registering to take the GRE. Otherwise, you can call ETS at 609-921-9000 and ask about registration fees and test dates. List the next GRE test date here:

5.   For most Ph.D. programs in I/O, you will need to complete the applications for admissions in December or January before the August in which you would like admission. Masters' program deadlines are typically later. You will usually need to write a letter of intention (or a personal statement) to include with your applications. It should be carefully typed, and should include information about your career goals and what you have done to prepare yourself for graduate school. You should be able to convince the person reading the letter that you are very interested in obtaining a graduate degree in this field, and that you are a qualified and motivated applicant. List some thoughts you will want to include in your personal statement here:

6.   You will also need letters of recommendation from faculty in your department. Ideally, you will have been working on research with at least one of your instructors, so that this instructor can write a letter saying that you have research experience. Be organized and ask for letters of recommendation a month or more before they are due. Provide your recommender with stamped envelopes with the appropriate addresses typed on them to facilitate the process. Make sure to provide your recommender with the dates that the recommendations are due. List three faculty members you may want to ask for letters of recommendation here:

a.

b.

c.

You have just taken several of the important steps in your process of considering and applying for graduate school. I wish you the best of luck with your decision about what you want to do with your future. It is important to think about your future career goals and how to prepare yourself to reach them. Consult your academic adviser with any questions you may have.

The following is a list of key terms and concepts as they are presented in Chapter 2. As a way to help you understand the chapter and get to know the material, go through each of the terms and describe them fully. Then compare your responses to the responses in the textbook.

Five steps in the Empirical Research Process (list them here):

Major Research Methods (list key characteristics, advantages, and disadvantages of each method below):

    a) Laboratory experiment:

b) Quasi-experiment:

c) Questionnaires:

d) Observation:

e) Computer simulation:

Secondary Research Methods

    a) Meta-analysis

    b) Qualitative research

    c) Ethnography

Measurement of Variables and Variables of Interest in I/O Research:

    a) Quantitative Variables:

b) Qualitative Variables:

c) Independent Variable:

d) Dependent Variable:

e) Predictor Variable:

f) Criterion Variable:

Levels of Measurement (describe and give examples):

    a) Nominal Scale:

    b) Ordinal Scale:

    c) Interval Scale:

    d) Ratio Scale:

Descriptive statistics:

Distributions and their shape:

    a) Frequency distribution (draw and describe):

    b) Normal distribution (draw and describe):

    c) Negatively skewed distribution (draw and describe):

d) Positively skewed distribution (draw and describe):

Measures of Central Tendency:

a) Mean:

b) Median:

c) Mode:

Measures of Variability:

a) Range:

b) Standard deviation:

The Concept of Correlation:

a) Symbol for correlation:

b) Range of correlation:

c) Positive correlation (define and give example):

d) Negative correlation (define and give example):

e) Size of correlation:

f) Scatterplot for two variables with a positive correlation:

g) Scatterplot for two variables with a negative correlation:

h) Correlation and causality:

Conclusions from Research:

Ethical Problems in Research:

Web Sites for Chapter 2

1) http://stats.bls.gov/proghome.htm

This web site deals with statistics that I/O psychologists might be interested in. This site is run by the Bureau of Labor Statistics. It has numerous statistics relevant to the labor force as well as access to a variety of surveys.

2) http://www.siop.org/TIP/Tipapr99/3Burnfield.htm

The SIOP salary survey can be viewed at this web site. This survey provides statistics mentioned in this chapter. It also illustrates the questionnaire method of research. In addition, you may find the survey findings interesting if you are considering I/O psychology as a career option.

3) http://www.pollingreport.com/Contents.htm

This web site reports the results of numerous public opinion polls, some of which deal with American business.

Name: _____   Date Due: _____

Exercise 2-1: Research Methods

DIRECTIONS: Following are examples of five studies related to industrial/ organizational psychology. After you read about research methods in your textbook, go through each of the five studies below and identify the research method, the independent and dependent variables, and consider how you might improve or expand upon the study that is described.

1. Available data still suggest that on average, women receive lower pay than men. A professor decided to design a program to train college women to negotiate higher salaries. To assess the effectiveness of the program, 30 college women were randomly assigned to attend either a 12-hour salary negotiation skill training course or to be on a waiting list for the course. After the first group attended the training, both groups were tested on their negotiation skills by a trained individual (a graduate student) role-playing as an employer making a job offer. The individuals who had salary negotiation skill training negotiated a higher salary in the role-playing exercise.

    Research method:

    Independent (predictor) variable(s):

Dependent (criterion) variable(s):

Weaknesses of this study or the method:

Can you think of another study the professor might want to conduct to further understand this issue? Explain.

2. A researcher wants to understand to what extent variables such as financial difficulties, employment commitment (how much work means to a person), social support, and an individual's ability to structure his or her time and keep busy have an impact on mental and physical health during unemployment. In order to answer this question, 100 unemployed executives are asked to complete a questionnaire that asks questions about financial difficulties, employment commitment, social support, time structure, mental health, and physical health. Forty of the 100 questionnaires given out are returned.

Research method:

Independent (predictor) variable(s):

Dependent (criterion) variable(s):

Weaknesses of this study or the method:

What other issues relevant to unemployment might the investigator want to study?

3. The Scandinavian Sweets Factory recently implemented shift work. The factory is now open 24 hours a day, and employees either work an early shift, a late shift, or a night shift. The manager plans to compare each shift in six months to assess whether there are differences in the groups on productivity and turnover.

Research method:

Independent (predictor) variable(s):

Dependent (criterion) variable(s):

Weaknesses of this study or the method:

What recommendations would you make for further research?

4. A researcher wanted to examine whether a new machine would lead to increased productivity on an assembly line at Sam's Office Supply Factory. He randomly assigned ten workers to the new machine and ten workers to the old machine. The workers in the two groups were carefully matched in terms of their ability and experience. The researcher monitored the total number of products produced and the amount of product rejects on the two machines over a period of two weeks. Results showed the workers on the new machine had higher levels of productivity.

Research method:

Independent (predictor) variable(s):

Dependent (criterion) variable(s):

Weaknesses of this study or the method:

Can we now assume for certain that the new machine is better? Why or why not?

5. In a study of bias in work performance ratings, Black and White undergraduate psychology students were assigned the task of providing work performance ratings for videotaped "employees" (really graduate students who were just pretending to be employees) who differed in terms of their race (Black or White). Level of work performance was held constant on the videotape. Results showed that White raters tended to give slightly higher work performance ratings to the White employees on the videotape. Black raters, on the other hand, tended to give slightly higher work performance ratings to the Black employees on the videotape.

Research method:

Independent (predictor) variable(s):

Dependent (criterion) variable(s):

Weaknesses of this study or the method:

Why might it be difficult to study race bias in work performance ratings in a real organizational setting? What variables would you lose control over?

Exercise 2-2: Analysis of Data

You have been hired to conduct a job satisfaction survey for a local gift shop that has 15 employees. You have given the 15 employees a job satisfaction survey, and you have calculated a job satisfaction score for each person. Total scores can range from 0 (very low job satisfaction) to 40 (very high job satisfaction).

The norms for this job satisfaction survey suggest that individuals who score less than 20 on this survey are dissatisfied with their jobs. Following are the scores for each of the 15 employees you surveyed.

Employee	Score
#01	40
#02	20
#03	8
#04	7
#05	10
#06	12
#07	38
#08	39
#09	10
#10	12
#11	15
#12	19
#13	21
#14	11
#15	18

$$\Sigma =$$

DIRECTIONS: Read Chapter 2 of your book, then answer the following questions using these data.

(1)   What is the average or mean job satisfaction score?

(2)   What is the median job satisfaction score?

(3)   What is the mode job satisfaction score?

(4)   What is the range of observed scores?

(5)   Draw a normal or bell-shaped distribution here:

       Draw a negatively skewed distribution here:

Draw a positively skewed distribution here:

Which type of distribution <u>best</u> describes the job satisfaction data?

(6) Can you draw any conclusions from the data you have collected (e.g., Are the employees satisfied or dissatisfied? What might be happening in this organization? What follow-up work might you do?)?

(7) Finally, let's say you decide to conduct a study on what variables are correlated with job satisfaction in this and other organizations.

    (a) What variables would you guess might be <u>positively</u> correlated with job satisfaction?

    (b) What variables might be <u>negatively</u> correlated with job satisfaction?

Exercise 2-3: Research Summary

This assignment involves writing a research summary. You will find a <u>research</u> article in a journal in the library. Then, you will write a short paper about the article. This assignment will help you to:

1) understand research methods used to study industrial psychology
2) become acquainted with research journals in psychology and business
3) improve your writing skills
4) learn more about a topic related to the course

Instructions: Find a <u>research</u> article (not a literature review) on a topic related to industrial/organizational psychology for the summary. Write a 4 to5 page double-spaced typed paper about the research article. Include the following information:

1) Purpose of the study
2) Methodology (e.g., subjects, measures used)
3) Main findings of study
4) Strengths and weaknesses of study (e.g., What is your opinion of this research? Does it interest you? Was it well done? How could the study be improved?)

Type your name in the top right corner of the first page. Number each page. Type the <u>complete</u> reference of your article at the top of your report in APA style (follow the format of your book's references and you will be fine). Cover the required information in the order listed above (purpose, methodology, findings, strengths). Include a heading for each of these sections. Staple a copy of the research article to your report. Do not copy sentences word for word from the research articles; this is plagiarism. You are to summarize the article in your own words.

<u>Eligible Topics:</u> The article you find should be concerned with a topic related to industrial/organizational psychology (e.g., job analysis, job evaluation, the validity of interviews, personality testing, honesty testing, training, performance appraisal, leadership, work motivation, job satisfaction, work-related stress). The article must report results of a study related to any of these topics. It should not be a review article. If you have questions about the appropriateness of a topic, ask your instructor.

<u>Finding an article</u>: You may want to use Psych Lit (ask your librarian for help) and search for an article on a topic of interest to you. You may also look through recent issues of I/O and business research journals to find a topic that is "eligible" for the summary. Recommended journals to look through include: <u>Academy of Management Journal</u>, <u>Journal of Vocational Behavior</u>, <u>Journal of Applied Psychology</u>, <u>Journal of Organizational Behavior</u>, and <u>Personnel Psychology</u>. (Be advised that none of these journals are accessible from InfoTrac.) Your instructor may suggest other journals. Some journal articles will be difficult to read and understand. You are not expected to be able to interpret complex statistical analyses and tables, but you should be able to summarize the article's main findings.

CRITERIA: STANDARDS
FOR DECISION-MAKING

The following is a list of key names, terms, and concepts from Chapter 3. First, read the chapter. Then, as a way to test yourself and to help you get to know the material better, go through each of the terms and describe them fully. Compare your responses to the responses in the textbook when you are finished.

Criteria:

Conceptual Criterion:

Actual Criterion:

Criterion Deficiency:

Criterion Relevance:

Criterion Contamination:

   a) Bias:

   b) Error:

Proximal Criteria:

Distal Criteria:

Deductive Approach to Criterion Development:

Inductive Approach to Criterion Development:

Job Analysis:

Three Major Sources of Job Information:

    a) job incumbent:

    b) supervisors:

    c) job analyst:

SME:

Task:

Position:

Job:

Job Family:

Task-Oriented Procedures:

a) Functional Job Analysis

Worker-Oriented Procedures:

a) KSAOs

Linkage Analysis:

Three Major Methods of Job Analysis:

a) interview:

b) direct observation:

c) structured questionnaires:

i)   Taxonomy

ii) Position Analysis Questionnaire (PAQ):

Dictionary of Occupational Titles (DOT):

O*NET:

Job Evaluation:

External Equity:

a) Wage Survey:

Internal Equity:

Compensable Factors:

Hay Plan:

Comparable Worth:

Equal Pay Act:

Standards for Criteria:

Objective Criteria:

    a) Production:

    b) Sales:

    c) Tenure or turnover:

d) Absenteeism:

e) Accidents:

f) Theft:

Subjective Criteria:

Relationship Among Job-Performance Criteria:

Dynamic Criteria:

Web Sites for Chapter 3

1) http://www.wave.net/upg/immigration/dot_index.html

   This is the web site for the <u>Dictionary of Occupational Titles</u>.

2) http://www.doleta.gov/programs/onet/

   This is the web site for O*NET.

3) http://harvey.psyc.vt.edu/

   This web site provides information on job analysis.

4) http://sol.brunel.ac.uk/~jarvis/bola/jobs/

   This web site also provides information on job analysis.

Exercise 3-1: Learning to Use the DOT

Have you ever stopped to think about how many types of jobs there are that people work at in the United States and in other countries? Have you ever met a candle wrapping-machine operator, a handkerchief sample clerk, or a snuff container inspector? In 1991, a revised fourth edition of the Dictionary of Occupational Titles (DOT) was published by the Department of Labor. The DOT contains job descriptions for over 20,000 occupations. Figure 3-1 below shows you part of the job description the DOT lists for Industrial/Organizational Psychologist.

The DOT also contains a wealth of other information, including information about the level of reasoning, mathematical ability, language development needed to perform adequately in the position, the extent of the physical demands required by a person in the job, and what level of education the job requires. The purpose of this exercise is to make you more familiar with the DOT and the information it provides. See the instructions on the next page.

Figure 3-1:

045-107-030 PSYCHOLOGIST, INDUSTRIAL-ORGANIZATIONAL
     Develops and applies psychological techniques to personnel administration, management, and marketing problems. Observes details of work and interviews workers and supervisors to establish physical, mental, educational, and other job requirements. Develops interview techniques, rating scales, and psychological tests to assess skills, abilities, aptitudes, and interests as aids in selection, placement, and promotion. Organizes training programs, applying principles of learning and individual differences, and evaluates and measures effectiveness of training methods by statistical analysis of production rate, reduction of accidents, absenteeism, and turnover. Counsels workers to improve job and personal adjustments. Conducts research studies of organizational structure, communication systems, group interactions, and motivational systems, and recommends changes to improve efficiency and effectiveness of individuals, organizational units, and organization. Investigates problems related to physical environment of work, such as illumination, noise, temperature, and ventilation, and recommends changes to increase efficiency and decrease accident rate. Conducts surveys and research studies to ascertain nature of effective supervision and leadership and to analyze factors affecting morale and motivation. Studies consumer reaction to new products and package designs, using surveys and tests, and measures effectiveness of advertising media to aid in sale of goods and services. (Job description continues)

GOE: 11.03.01   **STRENGTH:** L   **GED:** R6 M6 L5 **SVP:** 8   **DLU:** 77

INSTRUCTIONS:

Go to the library and find the most recent issue of the <u>Dictionary of Occupational Titles</u> (DOT; Department of Labor, fourth edition, revised 1991). This book is typically in the Reference section at the library, meaning that you cannot check it out, but you can look at it while at the library. It may also be found in the Government Documents section. The reference librarian at your library will help you if you have problems finding it. Choose one job you are interested in from the many jobs described in the DOT. Answer the following questions about this job. *Attach a photocopy of the job description you use from the DOT.*

1. *What is the DOT job title of the job you chose?*

2. *What is its 9-digit DOT occupational code? (see top left corner of description)*

3. The <u>first</u> digit of the 9-digit occupational code refers to the major occupational category the occupation belongs to, as follows:
   0 and 1 = Professional, technical, and managerial occupations
         2 = Clerical and sales occupations
         3 = Service occupations
         4 = Agricultural, fishery, forestry, and related occupations
         5 = Processing occupations
         6 = Machine trades occupations
         7 = Bench work occupations
         8 = Structural work occupations
         9 = Miscellaneous occupations

   The first digit in the occupational code for I/O Psychologist (see Figure 3-1), for example, is a "0," meaning it is a professional, technical, or managerial occupation.

   What major occupational category does the job you chose belong to?

4. Now please look at the 4th, 5th, and 6th digits (the middle three numbers) of the 9-digit occupational code. These numbers give information regarding what extent the job requires working with data (numbers, words, or symbols; 4th digit), with people (human beings, or animals if dealt with on an individual basis; 5th digit), or with things (inanimate objects; 6th digit). Lower numbers indicate a job that is more complex. For example, Figure 3-1 shows the job of I/O Psychologist is rated as complex on working with data (rating = 1) and people (rating = 0), but less complex on working with things (rating = 7).

   Look at the 4th, 5th, and 6th digits of the occupational code you looked up. *Does this job require a high, medium, or low involvement with data, people, or things?* Look in the DOT for a more detailed explanation of these three digits if you are interested (in the 1991 DOT, see volume 2, page 1005).

   Data:

   People:

   Things:

5. Now look at the numbers below the job description. To the far right, you will see the letters "DLU", or "Date of Last Update". This refers to the last year in which that occupation was analyzed for this publication. You can see in Figure 3-1 that the job of I/O Psychologist was last updated in 1977. *What is the DLU for the occupation you are looking at?*

6. To the left of "DLU" you will see "SVP." This stands for "Specific Vocational Preparation." This refers to the amount of time a typical worker takes to learn the techniques and information required on the job. Following are the different levels of specific vocational preparation:

> 1 = Only a short demonstration needed to learn the job
> 2 = Anything beyond a short demonstration to 1 month
> 3 = Over 1 month to 3 months
> 4 = Over 3 months to 6 months
> 5 = Over 6 months to 1 year
> 6 = Over 1 year to 2 years
> 7 = Over 2 years to 4 years
> 8 = Over 4 years to 10 years
> 9 = Over 10 years

What is the SVP for the occupation you have chosen for this exercise?

7. To the left of SVP at the bottom of the job description you will see "GED." The GED Scale has three divisions: Reasoning Development (R), Mathematical Development (M), and Language Development (L). The ratings tell you what levels of these skills are required for satisfactory performance in your job of interest. Scores on this scale range from 1 to 6. <u>Higher scores represent higher levels of skill necessary</u>.

Appendix C in volume 2 (page 1009) of the 1991 DOT provides a table that fully explains each GED Reasoning, Mathematical, and Language level. Look up this table while you are at the library and answer the following questions. (Note: you may be using an older edition of the DOT. If so, this table will still be provided in the book, but in another place. Please consult the table of contents.)

> a. *What is the reasoning level (R) for the occupation you have chosen for this exercise? Briefly summarize what the table says this means.*

b. *What is the mathematical development level (M) for the occupation you have chosen? Briefly summarize what the table says this means.*

c. *What is the language development level (L) for the occupation you have chosen? Briefly summarize what the table says this means.*

8. To the left of the GED rating is a rating for "Strength," telling us what level of physical strength is required for someone to perform well on the job. There are five strength ratings: S = Sedentary Work, L = Light Work, M = Medium Work, H = Heavy Work, and V = Very Heavy Work.

Very heavy work, for example, is defined as "exerting in excess of 100 pounds of force occasionally, and/or in excess of 50 pounds of force frequently, and/or in excess of 20 pounds of force constantly to move objects." *What level of strength does the occupation you chose to summarize require?*

9. The furthest rating to the left on the bottom of the DOT job description is the "GOE." These numbers provide further information about the job in the job description. Have you ever taken an interest test that assesses your occupational interests? The first two numbers in the GOE rating provide information about what vocational interests are accommodated in that job. The twelve major interest areas indicated by the first two numbers of the GOE are as follows:

01 Artistic	05 Mechanical	09 Accommodating
02 Scientific	06 Industrial	10 Humanitarian
03 Plants/Animals	07 Business Detail	11 Leading-Influencing
04 Protective	08 Selling	12 Physical Performing

What is the major interest area indicated by the first two numbers of the GOE rating for your occupation of interest?

10. Note that there is a wealth of information in the DOT. Hopefully this exercise has made you familiar with at least some of it. Now, one final question for you to ponder.

    What do you think is difficult about composing a dictionary such as the DOT? Can you think of any potential weaknesses of the DOT?

Name: _____   Date Due: _____

Exercise 3-2: Pseudo Job Analysis Project

This exercise gives you the opportunity to conduct a mini or "pseudo" worker-oriented job analysis. You will summarize the results of your job analysis in a typed report that you will hand in to your instructor.

You will derive your job analytic information from one employee in a job of your choice using the interview method. You should choose to interview an employee who works full-time (or over 20 hours per week) in his or her job, and who has worked in his or her job for at least six months. The interview will most likely take one hour or more. You may want to tape-record the interview. You should supplement the data derived from the interview with observational information (e.g., watch the person at work, visit the workplace, or look at samples of the person's work).

Your typed job analysis report should include the following five sections. Label sections 2, 3, 4, and 5 with a section heading. For example, you should have a section heading for the second part, labeled "Interviewee/Organization Information."

1. Cover sheet: Include a title (e.g., "Pseudo Job Analysis), your name, the date, the course number, and instructor's name.

2. Interviewee/Organization information: Include your subject's name (can make it up or use real name), level of education, tenure, and rating of job satisfaction (1 = I hate my job to 7 = I love my job). Also include the individual's job title and what the organization does that the individual works for. Include information about how big or small the organization is, and how the individual's job fits in with other jobs in the organization.

3. DOT Job Description: Go to the library and look up the person's job title in the Dictionary of Occupational Titles. You may have to experiment with different job titles. Type the job description you find listed in the DOT and the DOT code in this section of your paper. If there are two DOT descriptions that seem to fit, choose the one that fits best (and make a note that another description is close).

4. <u>Knowledge, skill, and ability statements</u>: Develop a list of knowledge, skills, and abilities (KSAs) needed to perform on the job (include 15 to 30 KSA statements). Write your KSAs clearly, be to the point, and do not be redundant. Sample KSA statements for the job of "medical technologist" have been included at the end of this exercise. After you have written your KSAs, you will need to meet with your subject one more time. First, have your subject review your KSA list for accuracy (have you stated anything that is not correct?) and comprehensiveness (are all KSAs represented?). Then have your subject rate each KSA on "How often is this KSA used on the job?" (1 = rarely used, 2 = sometimes used, 3 = often used, 4 = very frequently used). This section of your report, when finished, should include your final list of KSAs and the rating your subject gave each KSA.

5. <u>What I learned from this project</u>: Write at least three paragraphs about what you learned from this project. Include information about what you learned from meeting with your subject a second time (e.g., were some of your KSAs stated incorrectly?). Include overall information about whether you found this project to be useful or difficult. Then include at least one paragraph explaining why job analysis is important to Industrial Psychology and how the information you collected could be used. How do you think this pseudo job analysis differs from a real job analysis?

Other Tips:

* Prepare for your interview and arrive on time. You may want to start your interview by getting the information you need for section #2 of your paper. The main purpose of your interview, however, will be to get information about what KSAs are needed for a person to be a successful performer on the job.

* Don't imply you are evaluating the <u>worth</u> of your subject's job. Don't say anything like "Is that all that you do?" You might offend the person you are interviewing.

* Possible questions for your interview include: "What kinds of skills does a worker need to perform well in this job?" "Tell me what you do when you get to work each day" and "What skills or abilities does a good worker have that a poor worker doesn't for this job?" You can write notes as a person responds and form them into KSAs later. Clarify any occupational jargon a person might use.

* When you write your KSAs, make sure they are not too specific or too broad. "Ability to write," for example, is too broad. Does that imply a person should be able to write novels, poems, songs, business reports, or what?

Write any additional instructions your instructor gives you here, or in your notebook, so that you don't forget.

Example KSA Statements for the Job of Medical Technologist

Following is a partial list of the KSAs used in the job of medical technologist to give you an idea of how KSAs are written. Note that each KSA statement starts with the word "Knowledge," "Skill," or "Ability." You should include a list of between 15 and 30 KSAs in your report. To the left of each of your KSA statements you can include your subject's rating (1 = rarely used, 2 = sometimes used, 3 = often used, 4 = very frequently used) of how often the KSA is used on the job. Be sure to provide the rating scale in your report to tell the reader what the ratings are referring to.

_____ 1. Knowledge of immunohematology, transfusion therapy, and phlebotomy.

_____ 2. Ability to conduct blood supply inventory and make judgements of present and predicted blood supply demands.

_____ 3. Ability to evaluate donor acceptability through an assessment of current health status and an interview concerning disease history.

_____ 4. Skill in blood collection process, including arm preparation, phlebotomy, and preparation of collection bags.

_____ 5. Ability to recognize and react to possible complications (fainting, loss of consciousness) following blood donation.

_____ 6. Skill to use standard laboratory instruments (microscope, centrifuge, platelet machine, and cell washer).

_____ 7. Ability to detect malfunctions and perform minor maintenance on laboratory instruments.

_____ 8. Knowledge of laboratory testing procedures.

_____ 9. Ability to accurately complete routine, detailed paperwork.

_____ 10. Ability to work efficiently and quickly under pressure.

_____ 11. Knowledge of government regulations and guidelines concerning blood banks.

Name: _____   Date Due: _____

> # Exercise 3-3: Criteria,
> # Contamination, and Deficiency

Directions:

Complete the following exercise to help you to improve your understanding of the concepts of conceptual and actual criteria, criterion deficiency, relevance, and contamination. Assume that you are hiring a new secretary for your organization. You wish to assess the applicant's potential as a secretary. You decide you will test the applicant's potential with a computer typing test.

1.   What is your conceptual criterion?

2.   What is your actual criterion?

3.   Explain the concept of criterion deficiency. What is probably deficient about your criterion?

4.   Explain the concept of criterion contamination and give examples of criterion contamination that you may find when testing the applicant with a computer typing test.

5.   Draw and label a Venn diagram in the space provided below that expresses the relationship between the conceptual and actual criteria discussed in this exercise. It may help to review Figure 3-1 of your textbook.

Name: _____   Date Due: _____

Exercise 3-4: Internal and External Equity

A relative of yours recently cashed in on some big earnings in the stock market. He now
plans to open a chain of 10 new convenience store/gas stations in the Midwest. He plans
to hire approximately 14 employees to work in each store. For example, for each store he
thinks he will need the following employees:

- 1 store manager
- 2 assistant managers
- 8 cashiers
- 1 shelf stocker
- 1 part-time custodian
- 1 administrative assistant/bookkeeper

Your relative knows that you are currently taking an I/O psychology course. You and he
get into a discussion, and several thought-provoking issues come up. Read over the
section on "job evaluation" in Chapter 3 of your textbook. Then answer the following
questions, keeping the above example in mind.

QUESTIONS

1. How should your relative go about determining what wages to pay each position?

2. Are employees likely to be more concerned with internal equity or external
equity issues? What might happen if employees feel there is not internal equity?
What might happen if employees feel there is not external equity?

3.   What is a wage survey? Would a wage survey be useful in this instance?

4.   After talking to you, your relative considers doing a wage survey to assess what other convenience stores are paying their employees. Make a list of questions for your relative that he might want to ask other employers in the survey. For example, you would probably want more information than just "How much money are you paying your employees per year?"

5.   Can you think of any reasons your relative should avoid paying his employees too much over what other employers are paying?

Chapter 4: Study Guide

PREDICTORS:
PSYCHOLOGICAL ASSESSMENTS

The following is a list of key terms and concepts as they are presented in Chapter 4. As a way to help you understand the chapter and get to know the material, go through each of the terms and describe them fully. Then compare your responses to the information provided in the textbook.

Reliability (define):

Test-Retest Reliability:

Equivalent-Form Reliability:

Internal-Consistency Reliability:

     a) Split-half reliability:

     b) Cronbach's alpha or Kuder-Richardson 20:

Inter-rater reliability:

Validity:

Criterion-Related Validity:

    a) Concurrent criterion-related validity:

    b) Predictive criterion-related validity:

Content Validity:

Face Validity:

Construct Validity:

    a) Convergent validity coefficients:

b) Divergent validity coefficients:

Sir Francis Galton:

Cattell:

Ebbinghaus:

Binet:

Terman:

Speed versus Power Tests:

Individual versus Group Tests:

Paper-and-Pencil versus Performance Tests:

Ethical Standards in Testing:

Mental Measurements Yearbook (MMY):

Tests in Print:

Intelligence Tests:

"g":

Mechanical Aptitude Tests:

Sensory/Motor Ability Tests:

Personality Inventories:

     a) Five factor model:

Integrity Tests:

Physical Abilities:

Multiple-Aptitude Test Batteries:

Computerized Adaptive Testing:

Interviews:

a) degree of structure:

b) situational interviews:

c) "illusion of validity":

Assessment Centers:

Work Samples:

Situational Exercises:

    a) Leaderless Group Discussion:

    b) In-basket Exercise:

Biographical Information:

Letters of Recommendation:

Drug Testing:

Polygraphy or Lie Detection:

Graphology:

Emotional Intelligence:

Overview and Evaluation of Predictors:

Web Sites for Chapter 4

1) http://www.winway.com/main2/default.htm

   At this web site you will find a listing of unlawful employment interview questions.

2) http://www.workindex.com/

   At this web site you will have access to numerous staffing services available on the web.

3) http://www4.law.cornell.edu/uscode/29/ch22.html

   At this web site you will find information on the Employee Polygraph Protection Act.

4) http://www.library.fullerton.edu/er/mentalscope.htm

   At this web site you will be able to see a sample from the <u>Mental Measurements Yearbook</u>.

Exercise 4-1: Assessing the Validity of a Clerical Selection Test

---

Assume for the purposes of this exercise that you are an I/O Psychologist. You have been hired by the XYZ Cola Company to develop and assess the validity of a clerical selection test. The intent of the clerical selection test will be to test applicants who want a job as a secretary.

The XYZ Cola Company currently has 2000 secretaries on payroll. The company has learned from experience that it is very important to have qualified individuals in their secretarial positions, and that top clerical employees seem to require less training time, produce higher quality work, and get higher performance ratings. Yet they have never had a formal test to use for selecting new secretaries.

You complete a careful job analysis and find that there are four major components to the work done by the clerical workers at XYZ Cola Company. These components are as follows:

1. Filing
2. Recording and Checking
3. Written Communication Skills
4. Typing

You develop four tests to assess these skills. For example, Figure 4-1 shows an example of an item from your "Written Communication Skills Test." You decide to calculate a total score for each person who takes your test by adding his or her four test scores together.

Figure 4-1: Sample item from Written Communication Skills Test

---

Directions: Following are several sentences. The underlined part of each sentence may contain an error in spelling, punctuation, or capitalization. If the underlined part of the sentence contains an error, then mark the box in front of the change that should be implemented for the sentence.

The Federal Express package should arrive at <u>3:00 pm Wenesday</u>.

☐ 3:00 pm Wenesday

☐ 3:00 p.m. Wenesday

☐ 3:00 p.m. Wednesday

☐ NO CHANGE NEEDED

Based on the information given on the previous page, please answer the following questions. Chapter 4 of your book will also help you answer the questions.

1. What does face validity refer to? Is the item in Figure 4-1 <u>face valid</u>?

2. What does <u>content validity</u> refer to? How might you determine whether the clerical test you have developed has sufficient content validity?

3. Give an example of how you might assess the <u>concurrent criterion-related validity</u> of your clerical test. Please be as specific as possible.

4. How would you assess the predictive criterion-related validity of your clerical test? Please be as specific as possible.

5. What would be an acceptable validity coefficient for your predictive criterion-related validity study in #4? (r = ?)

6. How might you assess the <u>convergent</u> validity of your clerical selection test?

7. Finally, how might you assess the <u>divergent</u> validity of your clerical selection test?

Exercise 4-2: Exploring the Situational Interview

Introduction:

Many employers are now using a type of structured interview known as the situational interview. In a situational interview, applicants are asked predetermined questions that require them to respond to what they would do in a hypothetical situation related to the job of interest. The hypothetical situation usually involves some kind of dilemma or choice of responses. For example, in the J. of Applied Psych. (vol. 72), Weekly and Gier (1987) provide the following situational interview question for a sales position:

A customer comes into the store to pick up a watch he had left for repair. The repair was supposed to have been completed a week ago, but the watch is not yet back from the repair shop. The customer becomes very angry. How would you handle this situation? (page 485)

When the situational interview is used, the interviewer must ask every applicant the same list of questions in a standardized manner. A scoring key should also be available to score every applicant's answer. Weekly and Gier (1987) provide the following scoring key for the situational interview question listed above (e.g., see page 485 of their article). The response listed at the low end of the scale (1) is supposed to indicate a poor response to the question, whereas the response listed at the high end of the scale (5) is supposed to indicate a good response to the question.

> *1 = Tell the customer it isn't back yet and ask him or her to check back later.*
>
> *2 =*
>
> *3 = Apologize, tell the customer that you will check into the problem and call him or her back later.*
>
> *4 =*
>
> *5 = Put the customer at ease and call the repair shop while the customer waits.*

Assignment:

This exercise requires you to write a situational interview question and to develop a scoring key to evaluate answers to your question. Then you must administer the question to two friends or classmates who have not seen your questions. Finally, assess their responses.

1. Write a situational interview question for the job of a **women's shoes salesperson**. Remember that the question should pose a hypothetical situation that might happen on the job, then it should ask the applicant what he or she would do in that situation.

2.   Now you have to come up with a way to score answers to your question. Develop a
5-point Likert scale to score responses. On the low end of the scale (1), write what
you feel would be a poor answer to the question. On the high end of the scale (5),
write what you feel would be a very good or optimal answer to the question. In the
middle of the scale (3), write what you feel would be an average or mediocre answer
to the question. You can, but you do not have to, provide sample answers for
ratings 2 and 4.

1 =

2 =

3 =

4 =

5 =

3. Now administer the situational interview question to two different friends or classmates that have not seen it. Make sure to ask the question of each individual in a standardized manner. Make sure to pause without talking to allow the individual to think about his or her answer. You may restate the question if needed. Write down each individual's response below, and then score the answers.

    Individual #1 Response:

    Individual #2 Response:

4. What are your impressions of the situational interview? Would you, as a job applicant, like to be asked these kinds of questions?

Exercise 4-3: The Leaderless Group Discussion

Introduction:

A situational exercise commonly used in assessment centers is called the Leaderless Group Discussion (LGD). An LGD involves a group discussion (among the *assessees*, or the individuals being evaluated) on a hypothetical situation.

Trained *assessors* (individuals who are evaluating the individuals in an assessment center) watch the group discussion carefully and rate the individuals on several dimensions, such as ability to communicate. Many of you will have the opportunity to participate in an assessment center one day. Today you will participate in a class demonstration of the Leaderless Group Discussion. Some of you will be assessees, some will be assessors.

Directions:

Your professor will send five volunteers to the hallway to read over the discussion problem below. These people will be the *assessees*. They will have five minutes to think of some comments to share about the problem presented below. They will then come back and have a discussion in chairs arranged in a circle in front of the class. The remainder of the class should read over the rating forms (these people will be the *assessors*). Your professor will assign two different assessees for each assessor to rate.

Discussion Problem:

The Department of Psychology at Minnesota State University has been asked by the State of Minnesota to evaluate the undergraduate psychology program's effectiveness. You are a member of a committee that was quickly formed to come up with a proposal for the State about this issue. Your committee meets in five minutes. When you meet, your group should brainstorm and discuss the following:

(1) What does "program effectiveness" mean?

(2) What are some ways you could evaluate the program's effectiveness? Are these methods feasible? What are their advantages and disadvantages?

When your committee meets, you will have only 20 minutes to come to a consensus on 3 to 5 proposed methods to evaluate the Psychology program. Be specific. If you cannot come to a consensus, you may propose another meeting be held to discuss this further.

For Assessors: Rating Form for Leaderless Group Discussion

Please rate your two assigned assessees on the following dimensions on this scale:

1	2	3	4	5
extremely weak		average		exceptional

	Assessee #	Assessee #
1. Participation: Example: Individual was enthusiastic and made strong contributions to the discussion.	_____	_____
2. Oral communication: Example: Individual used proper grammar and vocabulary and expressed thoughts clearly.	_____	_____
3. Creativity: Example: Individual tried to brainstorm different possibilities to evaluate the program, or was able to think of several advantages or disadvantages.	_____	_____
4. Leadership: Example: Individual made sure the group was making progress, tried to get others involved, or demonstrated other leadership behaviors in the discussion.	_____	_____
5. Listening skills: Example: Individual seemed to actively listen to the other individuals in the group, clarifying their points when necessary.	_____	_____
6. Decision making: Example: Individual demonstrated a strong ability to make sound judgments and decisions.	_____	_____
Total Score:	_____	_____

The following is a list of key terms and concepts as they are presented in Chapter 5. As a way to help you understand the chapter and get to know the material, go through each of the terms and describe them fully. Then compare your responses to the information provided in the textbook.

Civil Rights Act of 1964:

a) Title VII:

b) Adverse Impact:

c) Disparate treatment:

d) 4/5ths rule:

e) Equal Employment Opportunity Commission:

f) "Griggs v. Duke Power Company":

g) "Albemarle v. Moody":

h) "Bakke v. University of California":

Age Discrimination in Employment Act:

Americans with Disabilities Act (ADA):

Civil Rights Act of 1991:

Recruitment:

Recruiting Yield Pyramid:

Bona Fide Occupational Qualification (BFOQ):

Affirmative Action:

Regression Analysis:

Regression Equation (Formula 5-1):

Multiple Predictors:

Venn Diagram of Two Uncorrelated Predictors:

Venn Diagram of Two Correlated Predictors:

Multiple Correlation ($\underline{R}$):

$\underline{R}^2$:

Multiple Regression Analysis:

Multiple Regression Equation (Formula 5-11):

Validity Generalization:

Three Major Factors that Influence the Utility of a Predictor:

a) Predictor Validity:

b) Selection Ratio:

c) Base Rate:

True Positives:

True Negatives:

False Negatives:

False Positives:

Determination of Cutoff Scores:

Banding:

Test Utility and Organizational Efficiency:

Placement:

Classification:

a) Vocational guidance strategy:

b) Pure selection strategy:

c) Successive selection strategy:

Web Sites for Chapter 5

1) http://janweb.icdi.wvu.edu/kinder/

   At this web site you will find the ADA document center.

2) http://www.careermosaic.com/

   This web site is an example of how many companies and many applicants are using the Internet for recruiting.

3) http://www.eeoc.gov/

   This web site is the EEOC home page. You can find a great deal of information pertaining to legal issues in selection.

4) http://www4.law.cornell.edu/uscode/29/ch14.html

   This web site by Cornell University provides legal information on the Age Discrimination in Employment Act.

5) http://www.eeoc.gov/facts/overview.html

   This web site provides an overview of the Equal Employment Opportunity Commission.

Exercise 5-1: Score Adjustments:
A Good or a Bad Practice

Organizations that use cognitive selection tests have found that Blacks and Hispanics often score lower (on the average) than Whites. The United States Employment Service (USES) encountered this problem when using the GATB (General Aptitude Test Battery) to test individuals seeking employment.

In the 1980s USES made a decision to calculate within-group percentages on the GATB. This means Blacks were compared to other Blacks taking the exam, and received a corresponding percentile score. Whites were compared to other Whites taking the exam, and received a corresponding percentile score. Because Blacks (on the average) scored lower than Whites, a Black individual with the same raw score as a White individual would receive a higher percentile score. This practice, known as *within-group norming* or *score adjustment*, was used to increase employment fairness. Without these score adjustments, only a small number of minorities would have reached the cutoffs needed to be recommended for job openings.

In 1991, the practice of score adjusting was outlawed by the Civil Rights Act of 1991. This Act states that employers cannot "adjust the scores of, use different cutoffs for, or otherwise alter the results of employment-related tests on the basis of race, color, religion, sex, or national origin."

As you might expect, the issue of whether score adjustments are useful, important, and legitimate as opposed to unfair and unjustified has been very controversial. Please think about this issue on your own or in a group, and complete the following questions.

1.   List all the arguments you can think of in <u>FAVOR</u> of score adjustments such as those described above.

2. List all the arguments you can think of in <u>OPPOSITION</u> of score adjustments such as those described above.

3. What is your personal opinion about the issue of score adjustments? Do you support the Civil Rights Act of 1991 in its prohibition of score adjustments?

4. What questions does this exercise raise in your mind about score adjustments or about the related issue of affirmative action?

Exercise 5-2: Understanding Adverse Impact

Adverse impact refers to when a selection method leads to a disproportionate percentage of people of a given group to be hired compared to another group. Your book describes how to decide if adverse impact is occurring. This exercise will help you to assess your understanding of adverse impact.

Assume for this exercise that you are a human resources director of a large organization. You are interested in assessing whether a certain selection procedure is leading to adverse impact among minorities. With this information in mind, please answer the following questions.

Questions

1. To assess the adverse impact of the selection procedure, you need to know the selection ratio for minorities and nonminorities. What information would you need to calculate the selection ratio (a) for minorities and (b) for nonminorities?

2. Adverse impact is determined by the 4/5ths rule. Explain this rule.

3. You have collected the following data for the selection procedure you are interested in. In 1996, 200 nonminorities and 45 minorities applied for a job with your organization. Using your selection procedure, 40 nonminorities and 6 minorities were selected. Based on this information, is there evidence of adverse impact? Write your calculations and reasoning below.

4. If adverse impact is found to exist, what should the employer do?

Name: _____   Date Due: _____

Exercise 5-3: Hooters and What is a BFOQ?

In Chapter 5 of your textbook, Field Note 1 discusses how a dentist who was looking for a partner could justify looking for a left-handed individual to join his practice, and thus not even consider hiring a right-handed dentist. Because the dentist was left-handed, and all of his instruments were left-handed, it was necessary for him to find a left-handed partner.

In Industrial Psychology, we call particular qualifications (such as left-handedness) that are enforced in hiring because they are reasonably necessary to the success of a business or enterprise "BFOQ's," or Bona Fide Occupational Qualifications. Another example of a BFOQ would be limiting your selection of a star for a documentary about Korea to an individual who is Korean. Although it is illegal to hire on the basis of race, being Korean may be a BFOQ when hiring for a documentary about Korea.

Following is an interesting article about a popular restaurant chain called "Hooters." At the time this exercise book was written, Hooters was in the middle of a controversy over whether or not they could justify hiring only women as waitresses. Hooters claims that being female is a BFOQ for their business. Read the newspaper article and answer the questions following the article.

EEOC call for male waiters is a drag, Hooters claims
By Bill Leonard (HRNews, December, 1995, Volume 14 (12), pp. 1-2) [1]

Hooters may be a restaurant where men go to play, but it's definitely not a place where they can go to work. At least that's what the Equal Employment Opportunity Commission (EEOC) claims.

The commission's complaints of sexual bias against the Atlanta-based restaurant chain have angered both the company's management and its famous "Hooter Girls" waitresses. Last month, Hooters went public with its fight against EEOC efforts to force it to hire male bartenders and waiters.

About 100 Hooters employees demonstrated along Pennsylvania Ave. in Washington, D.C. The women, clad in orange jumpsuits, carried posters and placards with slogans such as: "Men as Hooter Guys: What a Drag" and "EEOC, I like my job, let me keep it."

The restaurant chain also ran full-page ads in The Washington Post and USA Today picturing a mustachioed man dressed in the Hooter's girl uniform of form-fitting tank top (with falsies) and orange running shorts. Headlines said: "What's Wrong With This Picture?" and "The Latest from the Folks Who Brought You the $435 Hammer."

Hooters management says it is prepared to spend up to $1 million to kindle grassroots support for its fight against the EEOC. The company planned more rallies in Dallas, Atlanta, Tampa and Miami.

The EEOC dispute with Hooters began in 1991 when it brought charges of sexual bias against the restaurant chain, which has 170 restaurants nationwide. The EEOC identified approximately 1,400 male applicants who had been turned down by the chain for jobs as bartenders, hosts and waiters.

The commission proposed a five-year conciliation agreement that Hooters management rejected. The proposed agreement would:
- Open job categories of waiters, bartenders and hosts to men.
- Provide $10 million in back pay to the 1,400 men who had been previously turned down for the jobs.
- Develop an awareness and sensitivity training program.

Hooters management argues that its employment policy is necessary to maintain the restaurants' image and that the sex restrictions are "bona fide occupational qualifications" under Title VII of the Civil Rights Act.

"Hooters guys just don't make sense," said Hooters Marketing Vice President Mike McNeil at a press conference before the demonstration in Washington. "This doesn't make legal sense, this doesn't make economic sense, and– in light of the 100,000 case backlog at the EEOC– this doesn't make moral sense."

McNeil and other Hooters managers have likened their case to Chinese restaurants that hire only Chinese waiters or French restaurants that will hire only French staff. "There is only one restaurant where you can go and see a Hooters girl," he said.

The EEOC, however, has continued to dispute Hooters' position, and negotiations between the commission and the restaurant chain broke down in November. Hooters management then decided to go public with its campaign to thwart the EEOC proposal. In a Nov. 21 statement, the EEOC declined to debate the issue publicly but said, "We fail to understand what Hooters is seeking to accomplish through this expensive, well-orchestrated campaign other than to intimidate a federal law enforcement agency and, more importantly, individuals whose rights may have been illegally violated." The statement noted that some men filed a private class-action lawsuit last December in U.S. District Court in Chicago alleging discriminatory hiring practices by Hooters.

"At first glance, Hooters' defense does appear to be a pretty strong one," said Jack Raisner, a business law professor at St. John's University in New York. "But when you start to examine what a court will really focus on, whether the hiring policy is justified by bona fide occupational qualifications (BFOQ), their position may weaken some."

Raisner said Hooters has to prove that its business is based upon men coming to see the Hooters girls. It's easy to support a female-only BFOQ when hiring women as dancers or models, but the issue of women-only as restaurant servers enters a gray area, he said.

"Hooters would have to show that its business would be irreparably harmed if they hired male waiters," Raisner said. "And that could be tough to prove."

The restaurant chain claims that it does hire men for management positions, cooks and kitchen help.

---

[1] *Reprinted with the permission of HRNews published by the Society for Human Resource Management, Alexandria, VA.*

Exercise 5-3 Questions

1.   Summarize the position of the EEOC:

2.   Summarize the position of Hooters:

3.   Do you think that being female is a justifiable BFOQ for Hooters' waitresses? Why or why not?

Chapter 6: Study Guide

TRAINING & DEVELOPMENT

The following is a list of key terms and concepts as they are presented in Chapter 6. As a way to help you understand the chapter and get to know the material, go through each of the terms and describe them fully. Then compare your responses to the information provided in the textbook.

Three phases of skill acquisition (describe each phase completely)**:**

    a) Declarative knowledge:

    b) Knowledge compilation:

    c) Procedural knowledge:

Linkage between the type of competitive strategy an organization uses and its training practices:

a) Speed strategy:

b) Innovation strategy:

c) Quality enhancement strategy:

d) Cost-reduction strategy:

Pretraining Environment:

Assessing Training Needs:

    a) Organizational analysis:

    b) Task analysis:

    c) Person analysis:

Methods and Techniques of Training:

a) On-site training methods:

    [1] On-the-job training:

    [2] Job rotation:

    [3] Apprentice training:

b) Off-site training methods:

    [1] Lectures:

[2] Audiovisual material:

[3] Conferences:

[4] Programmed instruction:

[5] Computer-assisted instruction:

[6] Simulation:

    i) Psychological Fidelity

ii) Physical Fidelity

[7] Role playing:

Management Development Issues:

Derailment:

Cultural Diversity Training:

a) Melting pot v. Multiculturalism

b) Attitude change programs:

c) Behavior change programs:

Sexual Harassment Training:

a) Quid pro quo harassment v. hostile environment harassment:

b) Three models used to explain sexual harassment:

c) Physical attractiveness and sexual harassment:

360-degree feedback:

Mentoring:

    a) Four states of the mentor relationship:

    b) Two major dimensions to the mentoring relationship:

Transfer of Training:

a) Generalization:

b) Maintenance:

c) Relapse-prevention training:

Kirkpatrick's (1976) four levels of criteria:

a) Reaction criteria:

b) Learning criteria:

c) Behavioral criteria:

d) Results criteria:

    i)   External Criteria

Four dimensions of training validity:

a) Training validity:

b) Transfer validity:

c) Intraorganizational validity:

d) Interorganizational validity:

Web Sites for Chapter 6

There are numerous web sites devoted to training. The web sites listed below provide access to training suppliers, articles on training, training job opportunities, training services on the Internet, and/or other forms of training resources.

1) http://www.astd.org/

   American Society for Training and Development

2) http://www.tcm.com/trdev/t2.html

   Training and Development Resource Page

3) http://www.trainingsupersite.com/

   TrainingSuperSite

4) http://www.masie.com/fused/trlinks/trlinks.cfm

   The Masie Center Training Resources Link

5) http://www.trainingnet.com/

   The TrainingNet

Name: _____   Date Due: _____

Exercise 6-1: Planning a Training Program

You are the Training Director for a large company that sells office equipment. You have developed a wide variety of training programs for this company, and there is a course catalog that is circulated each year for employees.

Recently, it has come to your attention that a training program on listening skills would be useful for managers in this company. Several managers have identified this as a skill that they need to work on. Numerous employees have also complained that their managers do not listen to them very well, but instead jump to give their own viewpoints. You therefore feel that there is sufficient evidence that a training program on listening skills should be added to your course catalog, and you are now in the process of planning the exact content and format of this training program.

Planning a training program involves a lot of thinking and coordination. This exercise will ask you to think through several components of the new training program. Please answer the five questions on the following pages.

For Your Information

Personnel Decisions, Inc. (PDI), a large consulting firm based out of Minneapolis, has recently (1992) published a book titled Successful Manager's Handbook with many important tips for managers. The book can also be helpful to trainers planning training programs for managers.

A few of the tips available in PDI's handbook on listening skills include:

1. Avoid interrupting people and don't respond too quickly.
2. Reschedule conversations with subordinates if you don't have time to listen.
3. Ask questions when clarification may be needed.
4. Avoid doing other work while listening.
5. Pay attention to your subordinate's body language.
6. Use reflective statements to summarize your subordinate's message.
7. Use eye contact while listening, nod, lean forward, smile if appropriate.

QUESTIONS

1. Your first step should be to state the objective(s) of the training program. It will be useful to include the objective(s) of the program in the training catalog to make it very clear to employees what the purpose of the program will be. Stating the objective(s) will also help you stay on target when designing and evaluating the training program. State 1 to 3 primary objectives of your training program below. Take care to make your objective statements as specific and clear as possible.

2. Next, review the training techniques/methods described in your textbook. Which training method(s) would you want to use for your listening skills training program? Describe what the content of your program would include given your choice of methods. What advantages/disadvantages do you see with the methods you have chosen?

3. How many participants are you going to allow into each training session? How long will your training session be? Will you need to include breaks?

4.   How will you evaluate the effectiveness of this training program?

5. What other things must you think about when planning this training program? Make a list of other issues/details you must attend to or organize here:

Exercise 6-2: Mentoring at Proctor & Gamble

The profile on page 142 features information about Mike Copeland, a human resource manager who has worked in Training and Development for the past 8½ years at Proctor & Gamble. Proctor & Gamble is a large organization of approximately 40,000 U.S. employees based in Cincinnati that produces many well-known laundry, cleaning, food, and personal care products. In this profile, Mike passes on information about his job as manager of training operations. He also describes a mentoring program available to employees at Proctor & Gamble. After reading about Mike's job and the mentoring program at Proctor & Gamble, please answer the following questions.

QUESTIONS

1.   Have you ever had a mentor? What did this mentor do for you?

2. Most mentoring relationships are <u>informal</u>. An informal mentoring relationship might form when two individuals work in close proximity and/or when they share interests, or are brought together through job demands. Although informal mentoring relationships are more common, a growing number of organizations (like Proctor & Gamble) are implementing <u>formal</u> mentoring programs. What might be the <u>advantages</u> and <u>disadvantages</u> of a formal mentoring program in comparison to informal mentoring relationships?

3. How would you determine the costs associated with establishing a formal mentoring program? How would you measure the results of the program?

4. What are the difficulties and rewards of working as a Development Manager for a large organization?

Human Resources Profile

Mike Copeland received a B.S. in Political Science from Xavier University in Cincinnati, OH, in 1969. He now works at Proctor & Gamble (P & G) in Cincinnati as the U.S. Region Training Operations Manager. Mike is responsible for assessing the training needs of employees at P & G, and for designing training programs to meet employee development needs. While he sometimes delivers training programs himself, he often hires trainers to conduct the actual training workshops. P & G offers a number of different training courses to employees. For example, courses on interpersonal skills, assertiveness, diversity, oral communication, situational leadership, and listening skills are offered regularly. A full curriculum of business skill training complements the personal skill offerings. Prior to his current position at P & G, Mike had similar responsibilities for P & G's international business.

Like many other large organizations, P & G has developed what is known as a "formal mentoring program" to help their employees grow and develop professionally, and to encourage employees to pursue long-term careers within the company. In a formal mentoring program, employees are <u>assigned</u> to a mentor. According to Mike, the purpose of the formal mentoring program at P & G is to ensure that everyone who wants a mentor has access to one. Assigned mentors help their mentees develop an understanding of the company's culture and how to succeed, they provide career advice and input when asked, and they share information about people in the company and how the company makes decisions.

Retention and development of employees is particularly important to P & G, for they are a promote-from-within company. Although anyone in the company can be involved in the mentoring program, it was initiated to help "level the playing field" for women and minorities. An internal company survey had shown that women and minorities felt they were not receiving the attention they needed from company managers. The mentor program was developed to ensure these employees received the attention and development they desired.

Mike discussed the advantages of the mentoring program at P & G, saying: "When the mentoring relationship is sound, benefits to the company are immediate. Both people are enriched by the interactions that occur." He also said that a mentor can be a "sea anchor in times of stress" for mentees, helping them understand events as they occur, and helping them focus their energies on business results. The program makes employees feel valued, and that their personal development is important to the organization. He noted that there can, however, be risk involved in a mentoring program when a relationship does not meet the individual's expectations. In these situations, a person is assigned to a new mentor. P & G has made it clear that individuals are not evaluated on whether or not their mentoring assignments work out. If a mentee has to be reassigned, there are no negative consequences for the mentee or the mentor. Thus, the mentoring program has designed safeguards so as to get the best results possible, minimizing risk and maximizing the benefits to the business and the employees.

Exercise 6-3: Training Evaluation

Should a company spend thousands of dollars a year on a training program without trying to assess the effectiveness of the program? Let's say you get a position following graduation with a company that asks you to evaluate whether or not a particular training program is worthwhile. Would you know where to start? This exercise will help you think through the different components of training evaluation.

Instructions: Read the following training evaluation problem, then carefully answer the questions listed on the following pages. Before beginning, you should be familiar with Kirkpatrick's (1976) four levels of criteria for evaluating training programs (reaction, learning, behavioral, and results) as described in Chapter 6 of your textbook.

TRAINING EVALUATION PROBLEM

"Walstart" has recently designed a training program for their employees on

crime prevention. Employees will attend a two-hour workshop designed

to train them to watch for shoplifters. They will also be taught procedures

that should be used when identifying a potential shoplifter. You are called

in to help Walstart evaluate the effectiveness of their training program.

You decide to evaluate the crime prevention training program with all four

of Kirkpatrick's levels of criteria. You are now sitting down to brainstorm

how you can best go about doing this.

1.   First, describe how and when you will assess <u>reaction criteria</u>. Write at least three
     questions you would use to assess this level of criteria.

2.   Now describe how and when you will assess <u>learning criteria</u>. Give some
     examples of the type of questions you will use to assess this level of criteria.

3.   Carefully describe how and when you will assess <u>behavioral criteria</u>.

4.   Finally, how will you assess <u>results criteria</u>? What are some aspects of the training program that will have to be documented as expenses? What are some aspects of the training program to document that may result in economic gain?

DISCUSSION QUESTIONS:

1. Do you think training evaluation is important? Describe what you would say to the CEO of Walstart if you needed to convince him or her of the need to evaluate the effectiveness of the company's new crime prevention workshops.

2. Do you believe every level of Kirkpatrick's criteria (reaction, learning, behavioral, results) is important to include in Walstart's evaluation process? Do you think any of the four evaluation criteria could be left out of all training evaluations?

PERFORMANCE APPRAISAL

The following is a list of key terms and concepts as they are presented in Chapter 7. As a way to help you understand the chapter and get to know the material, go through each of the terms and describe them fully. Then compare your responses to the responses in the textbook.

Major uses of performance appraisal information (describe each use completely):

a) Personnel Training:

b) Wage and Salary Administration:

c) Placement:

d) Promotions:

e) Discharge:

f) Personnel Research:

Performance Appraisal and the Law:

Sources of Performance Appraisal Information:

a) Objective Production Data:

b) Personnel Data:

c) Judgmental Data:

Performance Appraisal Methods:

a) Graphic Rating Scales:

b) Rank-Order Method:

c) Paired-Comparison Method:

d) Forced-Distribution Method:

e) Critical Incidents:

f) Behaviorally-Anchored Rating Scales (BARS):

g) Behavioral-Observation Scales (BOS):

Rating Errors:

a) Halo Errors:

b) Leniency Errors:

c) Central-Tendency Errors:

Rater Training:

Frame-of-Reference Training:

Rater Motivation:

Contextual Performance:

Self-Assessments:

Peer Assessments:

Feedback of Appraisal Information to Employees:

Web Sites for Chapter 7

1) http://www.zigonperf.com/performance.htm

   At this site performance appraisal resources are available.

2) http://www.360-degreefeedback.com/

   This web site provides information on 360-degree feedback.

3) http://www.sfgate.com/cgi-bin/article.cgi?file=/chronicle/archive/
   1997/05/05/BU65200.DTL

   This web site is an article on 360-degree feedback.

4) http://www.apa.org/monitor/jul95/feedback.html

   This web site is an article on subordinate feedback in the appraisal process.

5) http://www.dutch.nl/bart/index.htm

   This web site is devoted to performance management.

Name: _____   Date Due: _____

Exercise 7-1: Employee Comparison Methods

This exercise will help you become more familiar with the rank-order method and the paired-comparison method of performance appraisal. You will rank-order and conduct paired-comparisons for the last six professors you have had. To start, please make a list of the last six professors you have had. Do not include the instructor for this course.

Professor A (Name):   Professor D (Name):

Professor B (Name):   Professor E (Name):

Professor C (Name):   Professor F (Name):

Using the Rank-Order Method: Rank the professors you listed above from "most effective instructor" to "least effective instructor."

    1.

    2.

    3.

    4.

    5.

    6.

<u>Using the Paired-Comparison Method</u>: Keeping in mind the names of each professor from the previous page, for each pair circle which professor you believe is more effective.

Professor A versus Professor B   Professor A versus Professor C

Professor A versus Professor D   Professor A versus Professor E

Professor A versus Professor F   Professor B versus Professor C

Professor B versus Professor D   Professor B versus Professor E

Professor B versus Professor F   Professor C versus Professor D

Professor C versus Professor E   Professor C versus Professor F

Professor D versus Professor E   Professor D versus Professor F

Professor E versus Professor F

Now count the number of times each professor was selected as the best.

A: _____   D: _____

B: _____   E: _____

C: _____   F: _____

<u>Evaluating the Rank-Order and Paired-Comparison Methods</u>: Did you find the same or different results when using these two different methods? What advantages and disadvantages do you see with each method?

Name: _____   Date Due: _____

Exercise 7-2: How Do You Rate?

Directions:

A.   Many organizations today ask individuals to complete <u>self</u>-ratings of job performance. Comparing yourself to other college students of your same age and class level, please complete the following self-ratings of your abilities.

1	2	3	4	5
Well Below Average		**Average**		**Well Above Average**

_____1.   Typing skills

_____2.   Ability to get along with others

_____3.   Writing skills

_____4.   Level of responsibility

_____5.   Friendliness

_____6.   Organizational abilities

_____7.   Promptness

_____8.   Energy level

B.   Add together your ratings for the 8 items and divide by 8. Write your computed

average for these items here: _____. Is your average rating above 3 on

this 5-point scale? What does the research on self-ratings say about how most

individuals in your class will rate themselves? Your instructor will discuss self-

ratings and this exercise with you further in class.

Exercise 7-3: How is Performance Evaluated at Your Organization

This exercise will give you the opportunity to find out more about performance appraisal in the "real world." You will be required to interview a human resources director or a manager who conducts performance appraisals of his or her employees. You will ask this individual questions that will help you to understand more about how his or her organization evaluates its employees.

Step 1: Visit an Organization

Identify a local organization that you wish to interview about their performance appraisal system. Call this organization and ask for a human resources director or for a manager. Explain that you would like to learn more about performance appraisal at their organization, and that you would like to schedule an appointment to meet with someone at their organization who conducts performance appraisals with his or her subordinates. When you meet with an individual from this organization, ask several questions that will help you learn more about performance appraisal at that organization. Following are a few sample questions to get you started.

1. What is your job title? How many individuals do you supervise? What do they do? Do you conduct evaluations with all of them?

2. How often do you conduct performance reviews? In your opinion, is this often enough? Too often? About right?

3. Do you have a standard form that you use to evaluate the job performance of your subordinates? Can I see an example of this form? (If a sample copy is not available for you to review, ask what dimensions of job performance individuals are evaluated on and what type of scale is used.)

4. What do you like about conducting performance appraisals? What do you dislike? Do you see a need for improvement in the performance evaluation procedures or forms used at this organization? Do the employees like the procedures used?

Step 2: Summarize Your Findings

Write a 2-page report detailing the information you gathered from your interview. Attach a copy of a performance appraisal form from the organization if they gave you one. Include the name of the individual you interviewed, his or her job title, and the name of the organization. Then, describe:

(a) The performance appraisal procedures followed in the organization or job you focused on (e.g., How often is performance appraised? Is there a standard performance appraisal form used to evaluate performance? How long is it, and what dimensions are included on it? What type of rating scale is used?).

(b) Advantages and disadvantages of the performance appraisal process used at the organization that you can see or that the individual you interviewed pointed out.

(c) Any additional comments and a brief summary of what you feel you learned from doing this exercise.

Other Tips:

- Prepare for your interview before your appointment and show up on time. Outline the questions you want to ask and be prepared to take notes. You may want to ask if you can use a tape recorder.

- You may decide to interview a manager or human resources professional at the organization you currently work for. The exercise will be most useful for you, however, if you are not already familiar with the performance appraisal system being used. If you are already familiar with the system at the organization you work for, it would be best to choose another organization.

- If you choose a large organization for this assignment, it will be useful to limit your discussion to performance appraisal of one particular job. For example, if you choose a hospital, you may want to limit your discussion to performance appraisal of the nurses at the hospital.

Chapter 8: Study Guide

ORGANIZATIONS and WORK TEAMS

The following is a list of key terms and concepts as they are presented in Chapter 8. As a way to help you understand this chapter, go through each of the terms and describe them fully. Then compare your responses to the responses in the text.

Three theories of organizations:

I. Classical Theory (main premise is):

a) Four basic components to any organization:

b) Four major structural principles

1) Functional principle:

2) Scalar principle:

3) Line/staff principle:

4) Span-of-control principle:

c) Main contribution of classical theory:

II. Neoclassical Theory (main premise is):

a) Attacks on the four major structural principles

    1) Functional principle:

    2) Scalar principle:

    3) Line/staff principle:

    4) Span-of-control principle:

b) Main contribution of neoclassical theory:

III. Systems Theory (main premise is):

a) Five parts of an organization:

b) Main contribution of systems theory:

Organizational Structure:

Coordinating Mechanisms:

a) mutual adjustment:

b) direct supervision:

c) standardization of work processes:

d) standardization of work output:

e) standardization of skills and knowledge:

Mintzberg's Five Basic Parts of an Organization:

a) operating core:

b) strategic apex:

c) middle line:

d) technostructure:

e) support staff:

f) centralization in relation to these five parts:

Re-organizing and Downsizing:

a) differentiate re-organizing & downsizing:

b) as it relates to Mintzberg's five basic parts:

c) consequences:

Components of Social Systems (define social system):

Roles (describe):

a) five aspects of roles:

b) role episode:

c) role differentiation:

Norms (describe):

a) four important properties of norms:

b) three-step process for developing & communicating norms:

c) means to attain compliance with norms:

d) norms and organizational objectives:

Organizational Culture (describe):

a) three key features of an organization's culture:

b) process by which culture is transmitted:

c) changing an organization's culture:

d) ASA cycle

Work Teams (describe):

Types of teams:

a) problem-resolution teams:

b) creative teams:

c) tactical teams:

Decision making in teams:

a) situation assessment:

b) metacognition:

c) shared mental models:

d) resource management:

e) team informity:

f) staff validity:

g) dyadic sensitivity:

Principles of teamwork (describe fully):

a) Teamwork implies that members provide feedback to and accept it from one another.

b) Teamwork implies the willingness, preparedness, and proclivity to back fellow members up during operations.

c) Teamwork involves group members' collectively viewing of themselves as a group whose success depends on their interaction.

d) Teamwork means fostering within-team interdependence.

e) Team leadership makes a difference with respect to the performance of the team.

Interpersonal processes in teams:

    a) communication:

    b) groupthink:

    c) trust:

    d) beneficial conflict:

    e) competitive conflict:

    f) cohesion:

Personnel selection for teams:

a) versus traditional approach for personnel selection:

b) five social skills critical for team members:

c) personality and team effectiveness:

Team Training:

Web Sites for Chapter 8

1) http://www.dmsp.dauphine.fr/Management/Management.html

This web site is an on-line journal called M@n@gement. It is planning to have an entire issue devoted to downsizing.

2) http://www.everestcg.com/

This web site provides information on creating and sustaining effective work teams.

3) http://www.workteams.unt.edu/

This web site is maintained by the Center for the Study of Work Teams.

4) http://home.ust.hk/~mnhulpke/piccul.html

This web site defines organizational culture and provides access to reports on organizational culture.

5) http://mars.wnec.edu/~achelte/grad12outline.htm

This is another web site devoted to organizational culture.

6) http://www.house.gov/democrats/research/downsize.html

This web site was created by the Democrats in the house of representatives. It provides access to articles discussing downsizing and our economy.

Exercise 8-1: Snak Pak Attak

Chapter 8 begins with the three major schools of thought about organizations: Classical Theory, Neoclassical Theory, and Systems Theory. The chapter then moves on to Mintzberg's five basic parts of an organization's structure. This exercise requires you to apply the main ideas from these theories to the following organization. Please read the following case study, then answer the questions following.

Snak Pak Attak Inc.[*] is the country's third leading producer of junk food. Some of its products are: Cauliflower Chips, Pimento Pretzels, Pepperoni Popcorn, and everybody's favorite Sardine Salsa Nacho Chips. To give you an idea of the company's influence in the U.S. junk food market, for the past three years the company has had sales exceeding 3 billion dollars and market shares ranging from 17% to 19%.

The company has not always been this successful. The company was founded by I. B. Leaveit in the early 1980s. I. B. took notice of the success of Ben & Jerry's creative approach to ice cream. He thought this strategy could work in the snack food industry. Of course, his products are much more unusual than anything by Ben & Jerry's. In 1982, he opened up a small factory in Iowa and began Snak Pak Attak. The company's motto is "Vegetable, Mineral, or Animal: Anything could be a snack food." It took a while for Snak Pak Attak products to catch on. By 1986, Sardine Salsa Nacho Chips became very trendy when Americans recognized the value of eating more fish. I. B. realized he had to expand his production facilities. In 1990, three newer and much larger production plants were opened in various locations across the U.S. In the early 1990s, Americans became concerned about reducing fat in their diet. The demand for Snak Pak Attak's Cauliflower Chips skyrocketed (only 2 grams of fat per serving). Further, Snak Pak Attak came out with a new healthy snack option, which had instant success: Brussel Sprout Baguettes. A thin crispy wafer with chunks of real brussel sprouts. Within the last year, Snak Pak Attak has added two more production facilities, doubled its sales staff, and has heavily automated its production line.

The company's organizational chart is in Figure 8-1 (p. 186). As you can see from the chart, I. B. is the CEO of the company. There are, however, a few aspects of the organization's design that are not evident from the chart. To begin with, under the vice-president of production operations there are 6 plant managers; one for each plant. There are 4 assistant plant managers for each plant manager. Further, each assistant plant manager is responsible for 10 foreman. Moreover, each foreman supervises 20 production workers. For the sales division, there are 5 regional sales directors: northeast, southeast, midwest, northwest, and southwest. Within each region there are 6 area coordinators.

Each area coordinator supervises 30 salespeople. Additionally, there are several positions which do not appear on the chart. There are clerical staff for each position from the foreman on up. Further, there is a considerable staff for each vice-president (e.g., human resource administrators, accountants, research scientists, marketing representatives). Security, custodians, mail clerks, and purchasing agents are also employed at each plant.

Job satisfaction at Snak Pak Attak is quite high, except for production workers. Production workers go through an extensive training program once they are hired. They are trained to do one highly specific job (functional specialization). Some of the production specialties are: bag fillers (fill package with exact amount of snack food), bag sealers (seal package), boxers, etc. It is quite common for production workers to become quite bored with their jobs in a relatively short time. The company did try to increase the production workers' job satisfaction by implementing an incentive system. The more units you produce, the larger your bonus will be. The program didn't work. Management failed to realize that production workers have an unwritten and unspoken code not to exceed the quota. The one production worker who did exceed the quota was "dealt with" discreetly by his co-workers. He surprisingly quit the week after he received his incentive bonus.

Overall, Snak Pak Attak is doing well in the fast-food industry. The company has several plans for the next few years. One change the company is going to make is to take advantage of NAFTA (North American Free Trade Agreement) by expanding their distribution into Mexico and Canada. Further, the company is going to introduce two more healthy snack foods to appeal to consumer demands (Cucumber Crackers & Possum Peanuts). Feel a little hungry?

*Please note that Snak Pak Attak is a fabricated organization. Any similarity to a real organization is purely coincidental and somewhat disturbing.

Questions:

(1) Classical Theory identified four main structural properties of organizations. Describe each of these properties as they apply to Snak Pak Attak.

    a) Functional principle

b) Scalar principle

c) Line/staff principle

d) Span-of-control principle

(2) Neoclassical Theory attacked each of the four structural properties identified by Classical Theory. Critique your response to question #1 using Neoclassical arguments.

    a) Functional principle

    b) Scalar principle

    c) Line/staff principle

d) Span-of-control principle

(3) Systems Approach views organizations as analogous to living organisms. Using Systems Theory concepts of stability, growth, and adaptability describe Snak Pak Attak.

(4) There are five basic parts to any organization according to Mintzberg. Apply each of these parts to this organization.

   a) operating core

   b) strategic apex

   c) middle line

d) technostructure

e) support staff

Figure 8-1

ORGANIZATIONAL CHART: **SNAK PAK ATTAK**

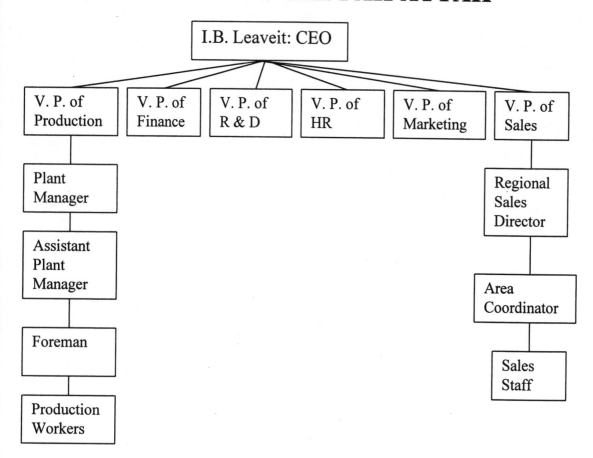

Exercise 8-2: Examining Social Systems

The next part of Chapter 8 examines the three main components of social systems: roles, norms, and organizational culture. The text defines roles as "the expectations of others about appropriate behavior in a specific position," whereas norms are defined as "shared group expectations about appropriate behavior." Finally, culture consists of "languages, values, attitudes, beliefs, and customs of an organization." As you can see these terms are quite similar. The way to differentiate among these terms is to determine the level of analysis. Roles focus on the *individual's position* (e.g., the role of a student). Norms pertain to *group* expectations (e.g., students in a particular class), whereas culture focuses on the *organization* as a whole (e.g., the student body of a particular college or university). By applying this knowledge to the following two scenarios, you will gain a better appreciation of the distinctiveness, interdependence and richness of these concepts.

Scenario #1: The Social System of your College/University

A) ROLES: the role of a student

1) What does your college/university expect of students in terms of:

a) a minimum acceptable GPA?

b) the proper way to address faculty?

c) the amount of time it should take to graduate?

d) scheduling courses for the upcoming semester?

2) Using Figure 8-7 from the text, describe a role episode that helped you learn an aspect of your role as a student.

B) NORMS: as it relates to this class

    1) What are the norms of this class in relation to:

        a) getting to class on time?

        b) participating in class?

        c) talking with the instructor before or after class?

        d) what is acceptable to wear to class?

e) other expected behaviors?

2) Go through your responses to the previous question by predicting what would happen if a classmate violated these norms.

   a) How do you think the instructor would react?

   b) How do you think the rest of the class would react?

   c) Do you think these reactions would prevent others from violating these norms? Explain.

3) The text points out that norms can vary considerably across groups within the same organization. Can you think of other classes you've had at this institution in which the norms were quite different? Explain.

C) CULTURE: of your college/university

1) What values/beliefs does your college/university try to instill in its students?

2) What ceremonies, rituals, or symbols are present at your school to communicate "the way we do things around here"?

3) Culture is considered both a cause and consequence of an organization's success or failure. When you think about a strength or weakness of your college/university, can you attribute part of the credit/blame to its culture?

Scenario #2: The Social System of your organization

For this scenario think of a company you work for or have worked for or an organization that you belong to (not counting your college/university) when answering these questions.

A) ROLES: as an employee

1) What role expectations does your organization have of you in terms of:

a) acceptable job performance?

b) proper attire to wear to work?

c) arrival and departure time each day?

d) communicating with superiors?

2) Using Figure 8-7 from the text, describe a role episode that helped you learn an aspect of your primary role as an employee.

3) Briefly describe all of the roles you assume in your job (e.g., worker, team leader, liaison to other departments).

B) NORMS: as it relates to your department/co-workers/shift

1) What are the norms in your department/co-workers/shift in relation to:

a) taking a sick day?

b) socializing with the boss?

c) taking lunch, coffee, or bathroom breaks?

d) speed at which employees work?

e) any other norms?

2) Go through your responses to the previous question by predicting what would happen if an employee violated these norms.

    a) How do you think the employee's boss would react?

    b) How do you think the rest of the group would react?

    c) Do you think these reactions would prevent others from violating these norms? Explain.

3) Finally, go through these norms one more time and determine if they coincide or contradict the organization's goals. For those norms that go against the objectives of the organizations, can you think of any ways to change these norms to comply with organizational goals?

C) CULTURE: of your organization

1) As the text points out "an organization's culture can often be traced to its founders." What values/beliefs did your organization's founder(s) try to instill? Are these still the values, beliefs, and attitudes today?

2) What slogans, ceremonies, rituals, legends, stories, or symbols are present at your organization to communicate "the way we do things around here"?

3) How has the external environment (e.g., technological advances, the economy, competition, legal developments) affected your organization's culture?

4) How has senior management tried to shape your organization's culture (e.g., hiring/firing, training, policies/procedures, communications) to adapt to its environment?

Exercise 8-3: Teams in Action

The final part of Chapter 8 examines the role of teams in the workplace. This assignment will give you an opportunity to work as part of a team as well as observe and evaluate another team's performance.

To complete this assignment, your instructor will divide the class into an even number of groups. Each group should range in size from 4 to 6 students. Half of the groups will be considered problem-resolution teams, whereas the other groups will be observing a problem-resolution team for scenario #1. For scenario #2, the groups will switch roles.

As observers you will watch the team interact. Then you will evaluate the team using the evaluation form on the next page. Please note that the evaluation criteria are directly related to the 5 principles of effective teamwork discussed in the text.

Scenario #1: Problem-Resolution

Your group has been given an opportunity to meet with the president of your college/university. The president would like your group to present to him/her the most pressing problem, from the students' view, this college/university that needs to be corrected. Your team has to decide what one aspect of the college/university you would like to change. Further, not only does your group have to agree on the problem to be changed, the team has to justify why it should be changed, how to change it, as well as the advantages and disadvantages in making this change.

Scenario #2: Creative Teams

You and your group are one of several research & development teams for Widget World Incorporated (WWI). Your task is to come up with a new product idea that will make the company millions of dollars. As you know WWI already makes a wide variety of unique products: the thermometer-turkey baster, the combo mechanical pencil & dinner fork (so you can eat while you work), glow in the dark golf balls, and the ever popular paper clip - nose hair clippers. Your team has to think of a *new unusual product* that would most likely be sold for less than $15, could be mass produced, and would sell to a large audience.

Teamwork Evaluation Form

Please rate the team you are observing using the following scale:

1	2	3	4	5
Poor		Satisfactory		Excellent

#1: *Teamwork implies that members provide feedback to and accept it from one another.*

___ 1. Participation from all team members was encouraged.
___ 2. Constructive criticism was valued rather than dismissed.

#2: *Teamwork implies the willingness, preparedness, and proclivity to back fellow members up during operations.*

___ 3. The team members took the initiative to help each other.
___ 4. Team members showed support for each others ideas.

#3: *Teamwork involves group members' collectively viewing of themselves as a group whose success depends on their interaction.*

___ 5. Team members seemed more concerned about the team's success rather than individual recognition.
___ 6. The team recognized that one member could not and should not "carry" the team in order to be highly effective.

#4: Teamwork means fostering within-team interdependence.

___ 7. Cooperation within the team was stressed.
___ 8. Every team member was viewed and treated as equally important to the team's success.

#5: *Team leadership makes a difference with respect to the performance of the team.*

___ 9. The team leader came across as a facilitator rather than a dictator.
___ 10. The team leader was able to provide and accept feedback.

___ **TOTAL SCORE**

Chapter 9: Study Guide

ORGANIZATIONAL ATTITUDES and BEHAVIOR

The following is a list of key terms and concepts as they are presented in Chapter 9. As a way to help you understand this chapter, go through each of the terms and describe them fully. Then compare your responses to the responses in the text.

Job Satisfaction:

a) Global job satisfaction:

b) Job facet satisfaction:

c) Withdrawal behavior:

Job Involvement:

Organizational Commitment:

a) Affective component:

b) Continuance component:

c) Normative component:

Organizational Justice:

a) Distributive justice:

1) equity rule:

2) equality rule:

3) need rule:

b) Procedural justice:

c) Systematic justice:

d) Configural justice:

e) Informational justice:

f) Interpersonal justice:

Organizational Citizenship Behavior:

a) Five main dimensions:

1) Altruism:

2) Conscientiousness:

3) Courtesy:

4) Sportsmanship:

5) Civic Virtue:

b) Dispositional origins of OCB:

c) Situational antecedents of OCB:

d) OCB and organizational justice:

Psychological contract:

a) Transactional versus relational psychological contracts:

b) The role of power in the psychological contract:

c) Consequences of violating the psychological contract:

Individual responses to organizational downsizing:

a) Terminated personnel:

b) Surviving personnel:

c) The use of contingent workers:

d) Overall advantages & disadvantages of downsizing:

The psychology of mergers and acquisitions:

a) merger versus an acquisition:

b) parent versus target organization:

c) integrating corporate cultures:

d) employee reactions to acquisitions:

Antisocial Behavior:

    a) Venting:

    b) Dissipation:

    c) Fatigue:

    d) Explosion:

Violence in the workplace:

a) Problems in identifying workplace aggressors:

b) Situational factors relating to workplace violence:

c) Strategies dealing with violence in the workplace:

Macro versus micro view of organizations:

a) Macro view:

b) Micro view:

Web Sites for Chapter 9

1) http://www.natss.org/

   This is the web site for the National Association of Temporary and Staffing Services.

2) http://www.osha-slc.gov/SLTC/workplaceviolence/index.html

   This is OSHA's web site for information on workplace violence.

3) http://www.inc.com/beyondthemag/between_the_pages/gallup.html

   This web site provides the results of a Gallup poll on job satisfaction.

4) http://www.itbp.com/hrm/iebm/commitment.htm

   This web site is an article on organizational commitment.

5) http://stats.bls.gov/news.release/conemp.nws.htm

   This web site is a report from the Department of Labor on the prevalence of contingent workers.

Exercise 9-1: The Scales of Justice

Chapter 9 begins with a discussion of organizational justice. More specifically, the chapter describes the various types of organizational justice: procedural, distributive, informational, interpersonal, systematic, and configural. The following case requires you to differentiate among these types of organizational justices by applying them to a case study. Please keep in mind that systematic justice and informational justice are types of procedural justice, whereas configural justice and interpersonal justice are types of distributive justice. Please read the following case study, then answer the questions following.

Black Mack Trucking Company is an interstate trucking company that transports a variety of goods and services. The company employs over 500 truckers. The company is experiencing a common HR problem. The turnover rate for truckers has gone up dramatically over the past 12 months. This increase in turnover corresponds to the time when the company implemented a new compensation system. Under the new system, starting salary is negotiated during the selection process. Previously, there was a set starting wage, which wasn't open to debate. The company is hoping to get new hires to agree on the lowest wage possible. Results, however, have varied based upon the negotiating skills of the new hire as well as the person's sex and racial background. The company is much more generous in bargaining when the new hire is female or a minority. The company is trying to avoid any clashes with the EEOC. Not surprising, the average starting salary for female truck drivers is $550 per week, for minorities it's $500 per week, and for White males it's $425 per week. Even though this practice violates the Equal Pay Act of 1963 ("equal pay for equal work"), the company is more concerned with increasing minority representation in their workforce. The company does not feel comfortable explaining their approach to determining starting salary. Thus, when an employee tries to challenge the system, the HR director simply states, "The company views salary as a private matter. We don't feel it is appropriate to justify perceived differences in starting salary. You agreed to your amount during the interviews. If you are no longer happy with your wage, it's unfortunate, but there's nothing we can do. If you don't like it, no one is stopping you from leaving." It didn't take long for employees to notice the differences in starting salary as well as the poor explanation by the HR director. Many employees quit right after the above mentioned spiel.

The new compensation system also covers bonus pay. The following memo was distributed to all truckers describing this new pay system.

Memorandum

To: All truckers

From: Marty Martin
           Human Resources Director

Subject: New Bonus System

Date: January 1, 1999

The company has decided to implement a new bonus system, effective immediately. The new system is designed to reward you for making deliveries on-time (within 1 hour of the scheduled arrival time). The company firmly believes that on-time deliveries are the key to repeat business, which in turn leads to a successful and prosperous organization. The more successful our company, the more we can reward you, our valued employees.

The system is quite simple. At the end of each month the percentage of times your deliveries were on-time will be calculated. Based upon your percentage, you will receive a bonus check according to the following table:

Percentage On-Time	Bonus for the Month
100%	$250
95 to 99%	$200
85 to 94%	$125
75 to 84%	$50
under 75%	$0

For example, if you make 20 deliveries this month and 18 of them are made on-time your percentage for the month would be 90% (18 divided by 20). You would receive a $125 bonus check.

If you have any questions or concerns, please feel free to give me a call at extension 310. I think this system will work to everyone's advantage!

At first glance, the bonus system seemed fair, however, the day-to-day operation of the system had several problems:

1) *Determining an estimated arrival time is very subjective.* For example, a delivery to Manhattan, NY takes much longer than a delivery to Manhattan, KS even if the mileage is equivalent. Also, a delivery at night is also less time consuming than at rush hour.

2) *Keeping accurate records of on-time deliveries is not simple.* Dispatchers now have to call every delivery site to check when the delivery arrived as well as maintain accurate records. The dispatchers felt they were overworked already. Numerous errors have been detected.

3) *The quality of the trucks vary considerably.* Some truckers have a lower percentage of on-time deliveries because their trucks break down. They feel they shouldn't be penalized for a flat tire or an overheated radiator.

4) *Safety is being compromised.* Many truckers are driving much more aggressively (e.g., speeding) to make sure they get there on-time. The number of accidents has doubled since the new bonus system has been implemented.

Since the new bonus system has been implemented, on-time deliveries has increased by 30%, however costs due to accidents and turnover have exceeded any gains.

QUESTIONS

(A) Starting Salary:

1) How fair is the starting salary system in terms of procedural justice?

a) More specifically, systematic justice?

b) informational justice?

2) How fair is the starting salary system in terms of distributive justice?

a) More specifically, configural justice?

b) interpersonal justice?

3) How can the company improve how it determines starting salaries?

(B) Bonus Pay:

1) Did the **memo** seem to indicate procedural and/or distributive justice? Explain.

2) Does the **bonus pay system** seem to have procedural and/or distributive justice?

3) Can the bonus pay system be improved and still motivate truckers to make deliveries on-time?

Name: _____   Date Due: _____

Exercise 9-2: The Good Soldier

The next major topic in chapter 9 is **organizational citizenship behavior** (OCB). OCB refers to going beyond job requirements and giving extra to the organization. The text mentions the five dimensions most often associated with OCB: altruism, conscientiousness, courtesy, sportsmanship, and civic virtue. This exercise will help you distinguish among these dimensions as well as illustrate the breadth of OCB.

PART 1: Your current or most recent job title: _____

> **List the top 5 task requirements of this job:** (keep in mind, this refers to things you were **required** to do; they should be listed in the job description)

1. _____

2. _____

3. _____

4. _____

5. _____

PART 2: OCB activities

Think of 6 behaviors that you do or did in this job that were not task requirements, but for the benefit of the organization (e.g., voluntarily joining committees). Then classify each behavior as either: altruism, conscientiousness, courtesy, sportsmanship, or civic virtue.

OCB Dimension   OCB Example

_____ 1.   _____

_____ 2.   _____

_____3. _____

_____4. _____

_____5. _____

_____6. _____

PART 3: Negative job behaviors

The text discusses OCB actions, which are positive influences on the organization. However, employees can also engage in other behaviors, not listed in their job description, that are detrimental to the organization (e.g., saying disparaging comments about organizational decisions). Basically, such acts could be considered anti-OCB actions. In this section, think of 6 examples of negative job behaviors that you have observed in your current or former job.

1. _____

2. _____

3. _____

4. _____

5. _____

6. _____

At this point it is pretty clear that employees can engage in numerous job behaviors, some of which have positive effects on the organization and some of which have damaging effects on the organization.

Questions:

1) When you think about how your job performance was evaluated, were these positive and negative job behaviors mentioned above included in your evaluation? If no, why do you think they were not?

2) How would you revise your performance evaluation to include these factors?

3) How much weight should be given to these factors in determining pay raises and promotions?

4) Can we really measure these positive and negative extra-role behaviors accurately? If no, are the above issues no longer valid?

Exercise 9-3: Power, Rage, & Anger

The last section of the chapter discusses violence in the workplace. As the text states, "the frequency and severity of workplace violence is escalating, both nationally and internationally." Thus, the importance of being prepared to handle workplace violence as well as implementing strategies to reduce workplace violence is critical. Listed below are two scenarios that deal with workplace violence. Please read each of the scenarios and then address the questions that follow. These scenarios should help you grasp the complexities of this volatile issue.

Scenario #1: "Frustrated, Fired Frank"

Frank Lee worked for Kirby Tires Inc. for the past 18 years. He started out on the assembly line making tires and was promoted to foreman around 6 years ago. Frank has a wife and three kids, two of whom are in college. Frank's job performance was excellent up until last year. Last Christmas his problems began. His parents left his house after Christmas dinner. On their way home, their car was blindsided by a drunk driver. His mother died instantly, while his father hung on for several weeks in intensive care before passing away.

Frank hasn't been the same since. The production rate of his line dropped off by 19%. He called in sick 13 times over the past 6 months. He was late at least 30 minutes every day for the past two weeks. Further, his attitude was very low; he never smiled, and seemed to be totally depressed. The company completely ignored the performance problems, because of his long productive history with the company. Nothing was even mentioned to him before last week. Late last week he received the following notice:

Dear Mr. F. Lee,

It has come to my attention that you have been repeatedly late in getting to work over the past few days. If this behavior continues, you will be immediately terminated.

Sincerely,
Kyle Rogers, HR Director

Frank came in late on Monday and Tuesday. Tuesday afternoon he received the following:

Dear Mr. F. Lee,

It has come to my attention that you have been repeatedly late this week as well. Your employment at Kirby Tires is terminated, effective immediately. All benefits you receive will be stopped by week's end.

Sincerely,
Kyle Rogers, HR Director

Frank did not handle the firing very well. On Wednesday morning Frank showed up for work, on time by the way, with a shotgun. He killed Kyle Rogers and then turned the gun on himself. The company is in shock.

Questions:

1) If you were the HR director, would you have handled the Frank Lee situation differently? If so, how?

2) What should the company do to reduce the likelihood of this ever happening again?

3) What steps would you take to help the company recover from such a tragic incident?

Scenario #2: "The customer is always right"

Violence in the workplace became a reality for Kloggy Klothes Stores. Marrisa Cupman, a customer, came into the store wanting to return a blouse she bought. The sales clerk, Jamie Johnson, asked Marrisa for her sales receipt. Marrisa replied, "I don't have a receipt. This was given to me as a birthday gift a few days ago." Jamie thought a moment of the company's return policy:
1. No returns without a receipt.
2. No returns if the merchandise was purchased more than 3 months ago.
3. No returns if the merchandise looks worn.
Jamie then took the garment from Marrisa's hand to examine it. Jamie recognized that the blouse was part of the company's own line of clothes, which just came out last week. The blouse looked like it had never been washed. Further, since the blouse is so new, its price had not changed.

Jamie handed the blouse back to Marrisa and said, "I'm sorry there's nothing I can do. No returns without a receipt." Marrisa became visibly upset and asked to speak to the manager. Jamie, not wanting to bother the manager, stated, "There's no one you can talk to. The manager is gone for the week. You'll have to come back then." Marrisa replied with numerous profanities. Jamie, upset by this reaction, reached into her pocket and threw Marrisa a quarter and said, "Call someone who cares." Marrisa threw the blouse in Jamie's face and increased her use of profanity. Jamie responded with similar comments and before long the two were fighting in the middle of the aisle. Other customers in the store were outraged. The manager tried to intervene, but it was too late. The damage was done. Marrisa has filed a lawsuit against the store for pain and suffering.

Questions:

1) How should Jamie have handled the situation to avoid such a conflict? Keep in mind she did enforce the company's return policy.

2) Are there any implications for human resources in terms of orientation, training, termination, selection or other I/O psychology areas to reduce the probability of this ever happening again?

3) If you were the store manager, what would you do for damage control? Many customers were visibly upset and about to leave the store upon seeing the incidence.

Chapter 10: Study Guide

STRESS and WELL-BEING at WORK

The following is a list of key terms and concepts as they are presented in Chapter 10. As a way to help you understand this chapter, go through each of the terms and describe them fully. Then compare your responses to the responses in the text.

Intrinsic value of work (define):

Instrumental value of work (define):

Environmental influences on mental health:

   a) Opportunity for control:

   b) Opportunity for skill use:

c) Externally generated goals:

d) Environmental variety:

e) Environmental clarity:

f) Availability of money:

g) Physical security:

h) Opportunity for interpersonal contact:

i) Valued social position:

The concept of mental health:

a) Affective well-being:

b) Competence:

c) Autonomy:

229

d) Aspiration:

e) Integrated functioning:

Work stress:

a) Organizational antecedents to stress:

b) Stressors in organizational life:

1) task content stressors:

2) role properties stressors:

3) role conflict:

4) role overload:

c) Perceptions & Cognitions: The appraisal process:

1) primary appraisal:

2) secondary appraisal:

d) Responses to stress:

    1) physiological:

    2) psychological:

    3) behavioral:

e) Consequences of stress:

f) Properties of the person as stress mediators:

    1) Type A personality:

2) Type B personality:

3) Internal locus of control:

4) External locus of control:

g) Properties of the situation as stress mediators:

1) Social support:

2) Other situational variables:

h) Prevention & intervention of stress:

    1) Prevention programs:

    2) Intervention initiatives:

Work/family conflict:

    a) The effect of work on family:

    b) The effect of family on work:

c) The family-work interaction:

d) Conceptual models of the relationship between work & family:

   1) Spillover Model:

   2) Compensation Model:

   3) Segmentation Model:

e) The relationship between work involvement & family involvement:

f) Organizational responses to reducing the work/family conflict:

1) Child-care centers:

2) The Family Medical Leave Act:

3) Elder-care programs:

4) Telecommuting:

Dual-career marriages:

    a) Effects on women:

    b) Effects on men:

    c) Lessening of temporal control:

The psychological effects of unemployment:

a) Intended & unintended consequences of employment:

b) Unemployment & discretionary control:

c) Relationship between unemployment & environmental determinants of mental health:

d) Middle-aged men & unemployment:

e) Women & unemployment:

f) Teenagers & unemployment:

g) The long-term unemployed:

Web Sites for Chapter 10

1) http://stats.bls.gov/eag.table.html

   Bureau of Labor Statistics web site that provides information on unemployment.

2) http://www4.law.cornell.edu/uscode/29/ch28.html

   This web site provides the text of the Family and Medical Leave Act.

3) http://www.welltech.com/programs/mmm.html

   This web site provides a description of a wellness program for 3M employees to help them balance work and family.

4) http://www.be-stress-free.com/

   This web site provides information on a stress management program.

5) http://www.hope.edu/academic/psychology/335/webrep/genroles.html

   This web site is an article on gender roles and work.

> # Exercise 10-1: "To Be or Not To Be" Employed

One of the most important sections of Chapter 10 deals with the psychological effects of unemployment. The following case study requires you to apply this material as well as discuss the implications of unemployment to an organization. Please read the following case study and answer the questions at the end.

You are the vice-president of human resources for a large manufacturing company. The company produces silverware. The company is able to manufacture approximately 12,000 table settings each month. The production process is relatively simple. Basically, all workers need to do is monitor various aspects of the system. They need to make sure there is enough raw material to produce the silverware. Also, they need to check for defects, work the stamping machine, adjust the rate of production, package the silverware, and load it onto trucks.

The company employs 600 production workers. Less than 5% of these workers have a college education. About 40% of them do not have a high school diploma. You suspect a considerable percentage of your workforce is illiterate. Additionally, most of your workers are male (85%) and over 40 years of age (median age = 43). The company is located in a relatively small northeastern city (population 25,000). The company was founded in this city over 80 years ago. The unemployment rate in the town is 7.9%, which is well above the national average. Your company is one of the few positive economic aspects of the community.

Unfortunately, the profits for the company have been steadily declining. Foreign competition and the increasing price of silver have lowered profits consistently over the past 10 years. Last year the company just broke even. If things do not change soon the company could be near bankruptcy within 5 to 10 years. The company's president has recently returned from a conference on technological advances in mass production. At the conference she learned about a new computer-automated production system. The system will be available in about 6 to 9 months. The cost of the technology is around $3 million; however, the new equipment could save the company about $10 million per year in reduced labor costs. If the company purchases the new technology, the company will be able to maintain production standards and quality with 350 fewer employees.

The president has scheduled a meeting for early next week for all vice-presidents to discuss the purchase of the new technology. If the company decides to acquire the new system, which you feel they most likely will, you will be in the unenviable position of laying off 350 production workers. You must be prepared to deal with this decision.

Questions:

1) How should the company decide which employees to lay off?

2) How should they be notified of the layoff?

3) How do you think the soon-to-be laid-off employees will react to the news?

4) How do you think the surviving employees will react?

5) Do you think the layoff will affect the community? Should this be a concern if it does?

6) Should the company offer workshops to the employees who will be laid-off to help them deal with the job loss and assist them in securing re-employment? What would be the content of the workshop?

Exercise 10-2: The Joy of Stress

*Another section of Chapter 10 deals with **work stress**; its causes, responses, consequences, and other elements related to stress. The following scenario describes two individuals who are experiencing work stress. Read the case and answer the questions that follow.*

You are the HR manager of a retail store that sells clothes for both men and women of all ages. The store has approximately 75 sales clerks. The store is open from 8 a.m. to 9 p.m. Monday through Saturday. On Sundays, the store is open from 10 a.m. to 6 p.m. The store is located in a large metropolitan area.

The first employee who has stopped by your office to complain about feeling stressed out is Jose DeMarco. Jose's job is relatively simple. When clothes arrive at the store, they are sent to Jose in a large bin with wheels. Jose attaches a theft detector device to every article of clothing. The device is the same for all the clothes. The device is applied rather easily. A piece of the clothing is put in a section of a large machine, Jose pushes a button, and the machine basically "staples" the security device. Once Jose finishes all the clothes in the bin, he gets another bin and starts over. Jose doesn't have to worry about problems with co-workers; he works completely alone. He is not supervised. His only requirement is that he must finish at least one bin per hour, which is somewhat demanding. As mentioned earlier, Jose works alone in a relatively small room. Unfortunately the room doesn't have any windows or air-conditioning. It does get pretty hot in there during the summer months. The air can be quite stale. Further, the room is noisy from the "stapling" machine. Jose claims the job has affected him in numerous ways: high blood pressure, ulcers, frustration and boredom. Jose is seriously thinking about quitting. You've also noticed from his personnel file that Jose has been absent more often this year than last, he's struggled on several occasions to meet his one bin per hour quota, and he has left work early 3 times already this year.

The second employee who stopped by your office to complain about job stress is Kim Chi. Kim is a sales clerk. Kim enjoys interacting with customers, working the register, maintaining a clean and orderly store area, and setting up displays. Kim has been trained to work in two adjacent areas of the store: women's sportswear and girls' formalwear. Kim often works in one section part of a given work day and the other section the other part of the day. There are different supervisors for each section of the store. Further, Kim's work schedule requires her to work three day shifts per week (8 a.m. to 5 p.m.) and two night shifts (2 p.m. to 9 p.m.). Kim has a difficult time getting along with the night supervisor of girls' formalwear. Kim thinks the tension is the result of the supervisor's prejudice towards Asian Americans. Another problem Kim has is that she often feels pulled in different directions. Some days she starts work in women's sportswear and the girls' formalwear supervisor tells her to stop what she's doing and work in formalwear. If she does move over to the formalwear, the sportswear supervisor gets upset. If she refuses, the formalwear supervisor gets upset. She often feels stuck-in-the-middle. Another complaint Kim has is that she feels the store is understaffed on the weekends. She often has a huge line of customers waiting at the register. Finally, Kim often feels overworked. For example, last Tuesday she started work at 8 a.m. A note was waiting for her from the supervisor. The note told her to redo all the displays in sportswear, and rack two bins of new clothes that came in yesterday before she leaves at five. Moreover, she was the only one scheduled to work that day in sportswear, which happened to be the last day of a sales promotion. Needless to say, she was swamped, and completely stressed out by the day's end. Not surprising, her displays were not as impressive as they have been in the past and her supervisor criticized her for them. Kim indicated that something has to change soon. She can't keep up this pace. She leaves work exhausted, often times with a splitting headache. Her morale is getting lower and lower. The other day she yelled at a co-worker, which she has never done before. This week she has been late twice.

Questions:

    1) What are the stressors for:

        a) Jose?

        b) Kim?

2)   The text mentions two types of stressors: task content and role properties.
       Which type fits with each person?

       a) Jose

       b) Kim

3)   The chapter mentions 3 types of responses to stress: physiological,
       psychological, and behavioral. Identify and then classify each response to
       stress into one of these three categories for:

       a) Jose

b) Kim

4) What organizational interventions would you recommend to help Jose and Kim to reduce/prevent or help them cope with stress?

a) Jose

b) Kim

Exercise 10-3: Love On The Rocks

The last sections of Chapter 10 deal with the difficulties of work, marriage, and family. The purpose of this exercise is to help you further appreciate the difficulties associated with work/family conflicts. Please read the following scenarios and respond to the questions below.

Scenario #1: Marc and Cleo

Marc and Cleo are expecting their first child in about five months. They have decided that one of them should stay home with the baby for at least one year. After the baby is one year old, the child will be put in day care. The trouble is who should stay home. Both of them are on the fast track to the executive suite. Their salaries are comparable. They know whomever takes a year off will have no guarantee of a job when they want to return to work. One of them will sacrifice their career development. If they split the year (six months each), both of them will sacrifice their careers.

Questions:

1) If you were in Marc or Cleo's position, how would you decide?

2) Do you think parents should sacrifice their careers for child-rearing?

Scenario #2: Bill and Hillary

Bill and Hillary are expecting their third child in a few months. For their first two children, Hillary quit work for five years to raise the kids until they were old enough for preschool. This time off hurt Hillary's career advancement as a graphics design specialist. Hillary has been working now for around six years and her career once again is about to take off. She is very excited about her career. This pregnancy, however, was not planned. Due to Hillary's sacrifices, Bill did quite well in his career. Currently, he is a junior partner in a CPA firm and he's the odds-on favorite to get the next senior partner position. If he takes off for an extended period (6 months or more) for this child, he believes the senior partners will see the move as a lack of commitment to the firm. All of the senior partners sacrificed family involvement for their careers, why shouldn't Bill? Senior partnership means much more money and prestige. Hillary and Bill agree that one of them should take time off to raise the child for at least a year, but who? Hillary feels she's sacrificed her career already and now it's Bill's turn. She wants a chance to be successful in her career. He has had his chance. Bill disagrees. Hillary's previous sacrifice has gotten him to where he is today. If he makes this sacrifice, he feels Hillary's sacrifice would be wasted. Therefore, Bill thinks Hillary should stay home with the baby.

Question:

1) Who should take off? Explain.

Overall Questions:

1) Should organizations ask applicants about their family responsibilities or intentions? Should this information be used to screen out applicants who may cause problems?

2) What programs or interventions could organizations adopt to reduce/eliminate the conflicts mentioned in the above scenarios?

3) Should organizations really care about family/work conflict? Should this really be a concern to a company? Explain the pros and cons.

4) How do you think organizational accommodations for work/family conflicts affect:

a) Organizational culture:

b) Organizational commitment:

c) Stress:

WORK MOTIVATION

The following is a list of key terms and concepts as they are presented in Chapter 11. As a way to help you understand this chapter, go through each of the terms and describe them fully. Then compare your responses to the responses in the text.

Work motivation (define):

    a) direction:

    b) intensity:

    c) persistence:

Five critical concepts

    a) behavior:

b) performance:

c) ability:

d) situational constraints:

e) motivation:

Work motivation theories

1) Need Hierarchy Theory

a) five needs:

b) empirical tests of the theory:

c) evaluation of the theory:

2) Equity Theory

a) four parts:

b) equity v. inequity:

c) underpayment:

d) overpayment:

e) empirical tests of the theory:

f) evaluation of the theory:

3) Expectancy Theory

a) job outcomes:

b) valence:

c) instrumentality:

d) expectancy:

e) force:

f) empirical tests of the theory:

g) evaluation of the theory:

4) Reinforcement Theory

a) stimulus:

b) response:

c) reward:

d) fixed interval:

e) fixed ratio:

f) variable interval:

g) variable ratio:

h) strengths and limitations:

i) empirical tests of the theory:

j) evaluation of the theory:

5) Goal-Setting Theory

a) two major functions of goals:

b) two pre-conditions for goal-setting to be effective:

c) factors that influence goal-setting effectiveness:

d) empirical tests of the theory:

e) evaluation of the theory:

Overview and Synthesis of Work Motivation Theories

a) distal construct theories:

b) proximal construct theories:

c) seven practices to raise motivation:

Application of Motivational Strategies:

Web Sites for Chapter 11

1) http://www.pmci.ca/text/motivation.html

   This web site is an example of a motivation workshop.

2) http://www.amazon.com/exec/obidos/excite-
   search/search%3Dwork%2Bmotivation/002-9458339-3563868

   This is a web site by amazon.com that provides books on work motivation.

3) http://www.np.ac.sg/~adp-aitac/TOPIC5/sub4c.htm

   This web site discusses a motivation theory not included in this chapter:
   McGregor's Theory X and Theory Y.

4) http://www.nwlink.com/~donclark/leader/want_job.html

   This web site is a motivation activity based on previous research.

5) http://www.shrm.org/hrmagazine/articles/0297sopa.htm

   This web site is an article from HR Magazine that discusses ESOPs as a
   motivation tool.

Exercise 11-1: The Performance-Motivation Relationship

This chapter addresses the various perspectives and complexities of work motivation. One of the most important points of this chapter is the relationship between performance and motivation. Too often people assume that your performance on a given task is the sole result of your motivation (you did well because you're a "hard worker" or you did poorly because you're "lazy"). As the text points out, there are other factors that influence your performance. Your ability to perform a task has a substantial impact on your performance. Situational factors (e.g., time limitations, poor equipment, reward system, leadership effectiveness, coworkers/peers) also influence your performance. Thus, performance is a result of your ability and your motivation, hindered by situational constraints. A mathematical representation of this relationship could be:

Performance = (Ability x Motivation) - Situational constraints

It's a multiplicative relationship because if one has limited ability (near "0") or almost no motivation (near "0"), performance will be almost nonexistent (near "0"). The highest performance will occur by an individual with high ability and high motivation and a supportive task environment (no situational constraints).

This exercise requires you to apply this formula to two situations. After completing the exercise, you should have a better grasp of the complexities in the relationship between performance and motivation.

Situation #1: This Course

At the end of this semester you will receive some grade in this course. The grade you receive represents your performance. Fill in the factors that will affect this outcome.

Performance in this course will be affected by:

**Which <u>abilities</u> are needed
to do well in this course?**　　a) _____

b) _____

c) _____

d) _____

**<u>Motivation</u>:
Why do you want to do well?**　　a) _____

b) _____

c) _____

d) _____

**What <u>situational constraints</u>
might affect your grade?**　　a) _____

b) _____

c) _____

d) _____

Taking into account the above information, what grade do you expect to receive in this course? Explain.

Situation #2: Your Job Performance

Think about your current job or a job you have recently been employed in. Your performance on that job was/will be appraised in some manner (either formally or informally). Fill in the factors that will affect or have affected your performance.

Job Performance (measured by): _____

Which **abilities** are needed
to do well on this job?

a) _____

b) _____

c) _____

d) _____

Motivation: Why do you want
to do well in this job?

a) _____

b) _____

c) _____

d) _____

What **situational constraints**
might affect your job performance?

a) _____

b) _____

c) _____

d) _____

Taking into account the above information, the performance evaluation you expect to receive in this job is (explain):

Exercise 11-2: What About Bob?

The majority of this chapter is devoted to the 5 main theories of work motivation: Need Hierarchy, Equity, Expectancy, Reinforcement, and Goal-Setting Theory. The following case study requires you to apply your knowledge of these theories. The goal of this exercise is to enhance your understanding of the major theoretical perspectives on work motivation.

What About Bob?

Bob Blakeslee is an attorney for the law firm of Lye, Cheet, and Steel. He's been employed with the firm for the past 10 years. When he started working there, he set a goal to become a senior partner before his 40th birthday. Last month he found out he's not going to accomplish his goal. The firm decided to promote Roberta James instead. The chances of another senior partner position opening up within the next 5 years are very slim.

Bob and Roberta started working at Lye, Cheet, and Steel at about the same time. Both Bob and Roberta graduated from the same law school, and had comparable academic accomplishments. Bob was told in his interview that promotion to senior partner would be based strictly upon how much revenue he could generate. Bob worked extremely hard to maintain a high number of "billable hours" per week. Bob would work 70 to 75 hours per week to maintain 50 to 55 billable hours per week (note: billable hours refer to time which a law firm can charge their clients). The firm charges clients $200 per hour for Bob's time. Roberta also desired senior partnership. She also put in comparable hours per week.

Bob took the news of Roberta's promotion pretty hard. Since the announcement of Roberta's promotion, Bob has been late to work 3 times. He's left work early on numerous occasions. His billable hours have averaged only 31 per week over the last month. To top it all off, one of Bob's new clients took his business elsewhere because he did not appreciate Bob's poor attitude. The loss of this client was estimated to cost the company $100,000 per year.

These recent developments in Bob's performance have not gone unnoticed. Brandon Cheet, one of the firm's senior partners, called Bob into his office to discuss these undesirable trends.

Brandon:	"Bob, we noticed your performance has slipped quite a bit over the last few weeks. Is anything wrong?"
Bob:	"I'm disgusted with my job. I can't believe I didn't get promoted."
Brandon:	"Bob, the firm has always been very impressed with you. We think of you as a valuable asset to our company. The choice between you and Roberta was very difficult. It was virtually a tie."
Bob:	"I have nothing against Roberta. She's a great lawyer. But I figure what's the point of killing myself. I work as hard as Roberta, but now she has the corner office, the company car, her name on the door, and the title. Why should I care anymore? It's probably going to be 10 more years before anyone else gets promoted."
Brandon:	"I'm sorry to hear you feel this way. The people here like you quite a bit."
Bob:	"I know they do. I have a lot of friends here. I really feel like I belong here, but I need more than that. The promotion would have meant respect. Plus it would have given me the opportunity for more challenging cases. I felt like the promotion was the ticket I needed to really become one of the best lawyers around."
Brandon:	"I'm sorry you didn't get the promotion, but I believe we made the right decision. The partners still value you very much, but if you don't get out of this funk you're in, you are going to force us to make another decision. So, please snap out of it before something drastic has to happen."
Bob:	"Sure."

Bob left Brandon's office. On his way back to his office, a co-worker stopped him and asked how the meeting went with Brandon. Bob replied, "It was a complete waste." Bob went home early that day.

Questions:

1) Which motivation theories are applicable to this case? Explain your answer.

2) If you were a senior partner in this firm, what would you do to increase Bob's motivation? Explain your response in the context of a theory (or theories).

3) If you were Bob, what could you do to increase your motivation? Explain.

Exercise 11-3: "To Know Thyself"

At the end of this chapter you should be quite familiar with work motivation. You should be familiar with the factors that affect motivation as well as the main theoretical perspectives on motivation. This exercise asks you to take a look at your own life and examine how motivation plays a role. The objective of this exercise is to show the value of the various motivation theories. Also, the exercise is intended to help you to develop an integrated view of motivation.

Part 1: Life Objectives: What is your primary objective (what do you hope to accomplish?) as a(n):

    a) **employee:**

    b) **student:**

c) family member:

d) friend:

e) citizen:

f) member of the human species:

Part 2: Applying the theories

a) Evaluate your goals based on your knowledge of Goal-Setting Theory. Are they specific, challenging, and attainable?

b) Equity Theory shows the impact of social comparisons. In coming up with these goals, do you think you were influenced by "others"? If so, who and how?

c) Reinforcement Theory highlights the value of rewards and punishments as affecting our behaviors. Do you think your past experiences (good and bad) affected these goals? Explain.

d) Need Hierarchy Theory suggests that motivation is the result of the desire to fulfill unconscious needs. Expectancy Theory, however, presents motivation as a result of conscious, highly rational thought. When you think about your behavior across various domains (e.g., work environment, at home, in society), do you think your behavior is guided by perceived expectancies and instrumentalities to accomplish the goals listed above or do you think your behavior is guided more by unknown/unconscious factors (possibly need fulfillment)? Explain.

e) Which of your goals does Expectancy Theory apply to the best? Which ones have the highest valence? Which ones have the strongest expectancy?

Part 3: Integrating the information: Based upon your responses to parts 1 and 2, create your own theory of motivation as it best applies to you. At the end of your theory indicate which theory or theories (if any) were most influential.

The following is a list of key terms and concepts as they are presented in Chapter 12. As a way to help you understand this chapter, go through each of the terms and describe them fully. Then compare your responses to the responses in the text.

Major Topics in Leadership Research:

a) Positional Power:

b) The Leader:

c) The Led:

d) The Influence Process:

e) The Situation:

f) Leader Emergence:

g) Leader Effectiveness:

Theoretical Approaches to Leadership:

a) The Trait Approach (list some key leadership traits):

b) The Behavioral Approach:

1) LBDQ

c) Power and Influence Approach:

1) Power and Leader Effectiveness:

    *Power Bases:

      a) reward:

      b) coercive:

      c) legitimate:

d) expert:

e) referent:

*Outcomes:

a) commitment:

b) compliance:

c) resistance:

* Gender Differences:

2) Leader-Member Exchange Theory:

3) Influence Tactics:

d) The Situational Approach:

    1) Path-Goal Theory:

    2) Cognitive Resources Theory:

Transactional and Charismatic Leadership:

    a) Transformational Leadership:

b) Charismatic Leadership:

c) Implicit Leadership Theory:

Substitutes for Leadership:

1) Self-leadership:

Points of Convergence Among Approaches:

a) Importance of influencing and motivating:

b) Importance of maintaining effective relations:

c) Importance of decision processes:

Cross-Cultural Leadership Issues:

a) Five key differences:

Diversity Issues in Leadership:

a) Impact of workforce diversity on leadership:

b) Gender differences in leadership:

Web Sites for Chapter 12

1) http://www.ccl.org/

   This is the web site for the Center for Creative Leadership.

2) http://www.emergingleadership.com/

   This is the web site of the Center for Emerging Leadership.

3) http://www.daggett.com/index.htm

   This is the web site of the International Center for Leadership in Education.

4) http://www.southwestct.dale-carnegie.com/

   This web site is for the Dale Carnegie Training program.

5) http://academy.umd.edu/Scholarship/CASL/index.htm

   This is the web site of the Academy of Leadership.

Exercise 12-1: Money, Money, Money

Prior to this year, the company you work for distributed a share of their profits with all of the employees equally. This practice, however, has consistently received numerous complaints from employees. A sample of these complaints are: "I've been here 30 years, I should get a bigger bonus than a new guy," "I'm a hell of a worker, why should a marginal performer get as much as me?" "I have three kids and two ex-wives to support, that should count for something," and "My job is very important to the success of this firm, why should I get the same bonus as every peon we employ in this place?" The company is getting fed up with these complaints. It has decided to create employee problem-solving groups to handle this situation.

You are part of one of these employee problem-solving groups. Most of the other groups have differentially weighted certain factors in their final awards, whereas a few groups have maintained the equal split. Your group has $10,000 to distribute among six employees. Your group decision will be binding for this year. The six employees are:

Billy Ray Roberts: 46 years old, salary = $18,000/year, 9 years with the firm, Custodian, married with five kids, satisfactory performer. He has grumbled numerous times about needing more money to support his family (good chance he would quit if he could find something better paying, which is possible).

Hilda Frummple: 63 years old, salary = $31,000/year, 38 years with the firm, Secretary, widow, marginal performer. She will be retiring soon. She loves the company, and employees adore her in spite of the fact she has not done a great job of keeping up with technological advances pertinent to her position.

Sherry Cordova: 27 years old, salary = $28,000/year, 2 years with the firm, Assistant Manager, single, excellent performer. She has been very impressive in her brief time in the company. She has the potential to move up quite rapidly in the company if she decides to stay (the job market, however, is quite good for her if she decides to look for employment elsewhere).

Simon Schuster: 54 years old, salary = $63,000/year, 27 years with the firm, Department Head, married with two kids in college, performance is debatable. The employees who work for him can't stand him. He is autocratic and verbally abusive at times. Turnover in his department is the highest in the firm, however departmental productivity is acceptable. He is a powerful individual within the firm; he is not the kind of person you want against you.

Carlos Menendez: 39 years old, salary = $35,000/year, 6 years with the firm, Computer Programmer, married, marginal performer, He is not well liked among his coworkers. Carlos believes this is because he is Hispanic. His wife is an attorney specializing in employment law. Carlos has a strong feeling that he is going to be discriminated against.

Lisa Cortland: 45 years old, salary = $40,000/year, 18 years with the firm, Manager, divorced, excellent performer. She has been consistently impressive. Her coworkers and subordinates think she is one of the best employees at the company.

Results:

After discussing the situation, what did your group decide? Be prepared to defend your answers.

Billy Ray Roberts	_____
Hilda Frummple	_____
Sherry Cordova	_____
Simon Schuster	_____
Carlos Menendez	_____
Lisa Cortland	_____
TOTAL	**$10,000**

Questions:

1. One of the key issues in this chapter is leader emergence. Did a leader(s) emerge in your group?

2. What traits do you think this person(s) possesses that enabled him/her to emerge as a leader?

3. In this situation, what traits and/or behaviors do you think are necessary for effective leadership?

4. The chapter discusses that in some situations appointed leaders are not needed. Do you think this class exercise needs an appointed leader? Explain.

Exercise 12-2: The Big Cheese

Chapter 12 discusses numerous important issues and concepts related to leadership. One of the best ways to learn about leadership, as well as most others areas, is through practical experience. This exercise requires you to reflect back upon your own experiences with a leader. By applying your experiences to the following questions you will gain a more thorough command of the key issues pertinent to leadership.

Part 1: Your Experiences: Think of a job you have had or a group that you belonged to that had a leader you respected. Keep in mind a leader could be anyone from the CEO of the organization, to your immediate supervisor, to a coworker, to a club president. Keep this person and this situation in mind as you answer the following questions.

a) Leader's job title: _____

b) Your relationship with this person (e.g., coworker, supervisor): _____

Part 2: Chapter Material

a) What **traits** does this person demonstrate that make him/her an effective leader?

b) What **behaviors** does this person exhibit as an effective leader?

c) Using French & Raven's 5 **bases of power**, which base(s) of power does this person rely on the most to influence others?

d) Which **influence tactics** does this person rely on as well?

e) Which **situational factors** affect this person's leadership style?

Part 3: Application of Course Concepts

a) Why do you think he/she was an effective leader?

b) Do you think this person would be an effective leader in most situations? Explain.

c) How important do you think leadership is to the success of an organization?

Exercise 12-3: Leadership & Learning

Chapter 12 presents numerous theories on leadership. This exercise is designed to help you further understand the similarities and differences among these theories by applying your knowledge of these theories to a situation common to the entire class. The common situation which this exercise refers to is the relationship between a teacher and his/her students, which does have commonalities to the relationship between a leader and his/her followers.

1) In what way(s) can a teacher be considered a leader?

2) A teacher could have at his/her disposal all 5 **bases of power** identified by French and Raven. Which bases of power do you think are most effective for a teacher to achieve desired outcomes (e.g., students learn, they are interested in course material, they perform well on tests)?

3) Apply the **Path-Goal** theory to the relationship between a teacher and his/her students.

4) The **Cognitive Resources** theory highlights the importance of intelligence, technical competence, and prior experience for effective leadership. Describe why each of these three concepts is critical to the job of a teacher.

5) When you think of your favorite teacher, would you consider this person a **transformational** leader or a **charismatic** leader? Explain.

6) Apply **Leader-Member Exchange** theory to the relationship between a teacher and his/her students.

7) Do you think a teacher's leadership style should vary based upon:

a) size of the class (20 v. 200)?

b) level of the course (freshman-level v. senior-level)?

c) course content (organic chemistry v. intro. to psychology v. poetry)?

d) student ability (remedial section v. honors section)?

*If yes, to any or all of the above, what does this tell you about effective leadership?

JOB DESIGN and ORGANIZATION DEVELOPMENT: CREATING HIGH PERFORMANCE ORGANIZATIONS

The following is a list of key terms and concepts as they are presented in Chapter 13. As a way to help you understand this chapter, go through each of the terms and describe them fully. Then compare your responses to the responses in the text.

To alter the worker or the workplace?

Job Design:

a) historical overview (Frederick Taylor):

b) job enlargement:

c) job enrichment:

d) task attributes:

e) Higher-Order Need Strength Questionnaire B:

f) Job-Characteristics Model (JCM):

    1) five core job dimensions:

2) three critical psychological states:

3) growth need strength:

4) motivating potential score:

5) personal and work outcomes:

6) empirical tests of JCM:

g) effectiveness of job-redesign programs:

h) organizational implications of job-redesign:

Organizational Development (OD):

a) Define:

b) Need for OD:

1) T-groups:

2) Organizational excellence:

c) Three basic concepts of OD:

1) The change agent:

2) The client:

3) The intervention:

d) Model of planned organizational change:

   1) Organizational work setting:

   2) Individual behavior:

   3) Organizational performance:

4) Individual development:

e) Typology of OD interventions:

f) Overcoming resistance to change:

1) Psychological ownership:

g) Employee empowerment

1) meaning:

2) competence:

3) self-determination:

4) impact:

h) major OD interventions:

1) Organizational culture change:

(i) 4 critical features of the change process:

(i) "back-sliding":

2) Total Quality Management (continuous process improvement):

a) Employee empowerment:

b) Statistical quality control:

c) Customer focus:

d) Business strategy:

i) Four keys to implement employee empowerment:

1) Sharing of information:

2) Developing knowledge:

3) Rewarding organizational performance:

4) Redistributing power:

j) ISO 9000:

k) Empirical OD research:

l) Values and ethics in OD:

Web Sites for Chapter 13

1) http://www.totalquality.net/

   This web site is devoted to total quality management.

2) http://www.exit109.com/~leebee/

   This web site is designed to help organizations achieve ISO 9000 certification.

3) http://www.itbp.com/hrm/iebm/job_design.htm

   This web site is a brief article on job design.

4) http://www.ethics.ubc.ca/start/bus.html

   This web site is devoted to business ethics.

5) http://deming.eng.clemson.edu/pub/den/

   This is the Deming Electronic Network web site.

Name: _____   Date Due: _____

Exercise 13-1: Has Your Work Life Been Enriching?

The most widely accepted theory of job enrichment is the **Job-Characteristics Model (JCM)**. As you may recall from the text, JCM has three parts: core job dimensions, critical psychological states, and personal and work outcomes. To help you further understand the nuances of this theory, this exercise requires you to apply the concepts identified by the theory to your own work experiences.

Step 1: Your most current job title: _____
If you are currently not working, select a job you held previously or a position you held within any type of organization (social, religious, volunteer).

Step 2: Core job dimensions
Based upon the job you selected in step 1, rate each core job dimension on a 1 to 5 scale in which:

1 = poor   2 = weak   3 = satisfactory   4 = good   5 = excellent

____ 1. **Skill Variety**:   the extent to which this job allowed you to do a number of different activities or use a number of different skills

____ 2. **Task Identity**:   the degree to which the job required you to complete a whole, identifiable piece of work (from beginning to end with visible results)

____ 3. **Task Significance:** the degree to which the job had an impact on the lives or work of other people within or outside the organization

____ 4. **Autonomy**:   the degree to which the job gave you freedom, independence, and discretion in scheduling the work and determining procedures to do the job

____ 5. **Task Feedback:**   the degree to which carrying out the activities required results in direct and clear information about the effectiveness of performance

319

Step 3: Motivating Potential Score: calculate the MPS of the job you selected

$$MPS = \frac{variety + task\ identity + task\ significance}{3} \times autonomy \times feedback$$

$$MPS = \underline{\qquad}$$

Step 4: Three Critical Psychological States

Using the scale below, evaluate the critical psychological states you experienced working at the selected job:

1 = poor   2 = weak   3 = satisfactory   4 = good   5 = excellent

___ 1. **Experienced meaningfulness of work:**   extent to which you felt the job was meaningful to you

___ 2. **Experienced responsibility for work outcomes:**   extent to which you felt you were responsible for work results

___ 3. **Knowledge of actual results of work activities:**   extent to which you felt you were informed of how well you were performing

Step 5: Personal and Work Outcomes

Using the scale below, evaluate the personal and work outcomes you got out of the selected job:

1 = poor   2 = weak   3 = satisfactory   4 = good   5 = excellent

___ 1. **Internal work motivation:** the extent to which you worked hard at this job because you enjoyed the work itself

___ 2. **Quality of work performed:** the extent of the quality of your work

___ 3. **Satisfaction with work:** the extent to which you enjoyed this job

___ 4. **Absenteeism and turnover:** the extent to which your attendance and desire to remain in the job was/is affected by the nature of the job

Step 6: Questions

1. Do you think employee **growth need strength** moderates the relationship between the three parts of this theory?

2. Based upon this exercise, would you recommend **job redesign** for the job you selected? Explain.

3. After applying this theory to your own work experience (as well as obtaining information from others), what do you see as the strengths and weaknesses of this theory?

Exercise 13-2: McBoring, McMonotony, McTurnover

Fast Freddy's Hamburger Emporium (a fictitious organization) prides itself on speedy service. Customers are guaranteed a hot meal within 5 minutes of their order. To meet this promise Fast Freddy's organizes the work flow based on work simplification and standardization. Each employee has a specialized function. Each store has: a hamburger flipper, a bun toaster, a french fryer, a condiment squirter, a food wrapper, a shake maker, etc. Each employee is hired to do one of these jobs and to do it very well and very fast. The company believes that if you hire and train employees to do one thing properly and quickly there will not be any accidents, bottlenecks, or errors. The company has determined that if everyone does their job correctly and efficiently, 24 hamburgers with fries can be ready to serve to the customer within 3.2 minutes.

Unfortunately, Fast Freddy's does not operate as efficiently as it would like. They have plenty of employee disciplinary problems. Lateness and absenteeism are above industry norms. Turnover runs at 200%, which is double the fast-food industry average. The average tenure is only six months. An even bigger employee problem is horseplay. Managers are constantly trying to stop employees from playing with the food they are supposed to be cooking. Food fights often happen when the manager leaves the cooking area. When employees are asked about how they feel about their job, the most common response is "bored." Management has tried to send employees for additional job training, but the trainers always say the same thing, "Employees know how to do their job, they just don't like doing it." Since additional training didn't work, the company tried increasing the starting salary for the job from minimum wage to $5.45 an hour with an additional $1 per hour increase after one year of service. Virtually no one, however, ever lasts a whole year. The increase in starting salary helped with recruiting, but it had no effect on retention.

1. What is the underlying problem for Fast Freddy's?

2. What are the financial consequences of this problem?

3. What would you recommend the company do to solve this problem?

4. What are the implications of your solution in terms of selection, training, compensation and other areas relevant to I/O psychology?

Exercise 13-3: "Quality is Job 1"

This chapter described two major organizational development interventions: organizational culture change and total quality management (TQM). This exercise deals with the latter. TQM is a very broad term that has received considerable attention in today's business world. One of the objectives of this chapter is to have you gain a full understanding of TQM. This exercise will help achieve this goal by having you apply TQM concepts to a variety of organizational scenarios.

One of the central concepts of TQM is to have a **customer focus** in your organization. One of the best ways to be customer focused is to provide a **quality** product or service. When organizations implement TQM, they identify indicators of quality in their product or service. These indicators need to be quantifiable. After the quality indicators are identified, then they are assessed statistically. The mean and variance of the indicators are computed. In TQM terms, this process is referred to as **statistical quality control**. The goal of TQM (continuous improvement) is to increase the mean value on the quality indicator (which translates to increasing the quality of the product or service) and to decrease the variance (so the quality of the product or service is consistent). Thus, at the end this process results in customers consistently receiving a high-quality product or service.

Based upon the above information as well as the information from this chapter, apply your knowledge of TQM to the following three scenarios:

Scenario #1: a car manufacturer (As you know there are many cars to choose within almost any price range, and the quality of the car could be the deciding factor to buy or not to buy.)

1. Identify a **quality** indicator for a car manufacturer (e.g., Ford Motor Co.) that is quantifiable.

2. Most likely there will be some variability across vehicles on your measure chosen (**variance**). What are two possible reasons for this variance?

3. Can **employee empowerment** (another central TQM concept) help reduce this variance or increase the mean on this indicator? Explain.

4. **Business strategy** is also crucial in TQM. Can you think of any changes in the business operations (e.g., technology, culture, training) that can help improve the quality of the automobile? Explain.

Scenario #2: a hotel (Similar to the above scenario, there are plenty of hotel options for customers. The quality of their stay can determine if they ever use that hotel again.)

1. Identify a **quality** indicator for a hotel (e.g., Hilton) that is quantifiable.

2. Most likely there will be some variability in the service provided to hotel customers on your chosen measure (**variance**). What are two possible reasons for this variance?

3. Can **employee empowerment** help reduce this variance or increase the mean on this indicator? Explain.

4. **Business strategy** is also crucial in TQM. Can you think of any changes in the business operations (e.g., technology, culture, training) that can help improve the quality of customer service for the hotel? Explain.

Scenario #3: a college or university (As a student, you are hoping that you are paying for a quality education. How does the institution know it is providing a quality learning experience?)

1. Identify a **quality** indicator for a college or university that is quantifiable:

2. Was this quality indicator something you thought about before you decided to enroll at your college or university? If no, do you wish you would have now?

3. Most likely there will be some variability in your chosen measure (**variance**). What are two possible reasons for this variance?

4. Can **employee empowerment** help reduce this variance or increase the mean on this indicator? Explain.

5. **Business strategy** is also crucial in TQM. Can you think of any changes in the business operations (e.g., technology, culture, training) that can help improve the quality of the education provided by this institution? Explain.

Chapter 14: Study Guide

UNION/MANAGEMENT RELATIONS

The following is a list of key terms and concepts as they are presented in Chapter 14. As a way to help you understand this chapter, go through each of the terms and describe them fully. Then compare your responses to the responses in the text.

The relationship between I/O psychology and union/management relations:

Union:

a) define:

b) advantages of unions to employees:

Unions as organizations:

a) large unions in the U.S.:

b) local union v. national union:

c) shop steward:

d) union dues:

The formation of a union:

a) union solicitation:

b) authorization cards:

c) National Labor Relations Board (NLRB):

d) union election:

e) union instrumentality:

The labor contract:

a) FIVE key issues:

b) negotiating the contract:

c) bargaining zone:

d) the role of external factors:

Collective bargaining and impasse resolution:

a) distributive bargaining:

b) integrative bargaining:

c) mediation:

1) Federal Mediation and Conciliation Service (FMCS):

d) fact-finding:

e) arbitration:

1) American Arbitration Association (AAA):

2) voluntary arbitration:

3) compulsory arbitration:

4) conventional arbitration:

5) final-offer arbitration:

Responses to impasse:

    a) union responses:

        1) strikes:

        2) work slowdowns:

        3) sabotage:

b) management responses:

   1) lockout:

Grievances:

   a) grievance arbitration:

   b) factors affecting filing of grievances:

Influence of unions on nonunionized companies:

Behavioral research on union/management relations:

a) employee support for collective bargaining:

b) union influence:

1) institutional socialization:

2) individual socialization:

c) dispute settlement:

d) commitment to the union:

1) Four-cell classification model:

I/O psychology and industrial relations:

    a) personnel selection:

        1) union shops:

        2) open and agency shops:

        3) union influence:

b) personnel training:

1) apprenticeship:

c) leadership development:

d) employee involvement:

Web Sites for Chapter 14

1) http://www.aflcio.org/

   This is the web site for the AFL-CIO.

2) http://www.nlrb.gov/

   This is the web site for the National Labor Relations Board.

3) http://www.ilr.cornell.edu/

   This is the web site for Cornell's Industrial Labor Relations program.

4) http://www.jtuc-rengo.or.jp/english/

   This is the web site for the Japanese Trade Union Confederation.

5) http://www.teamster.org/

   This is the Teamster's web site.

6) http://www.uaw.org/

   This is the web site for the United Auto Workers.

Exercise 14-1: Wheelin' & Dealin'

This exercise will give you a small taste of union/management negotiations. Your instructor will assign you to either role-play a union negotiator or a management negotiator. You will bargain over four issues that are typically discussed in collective bargaining. There are two conditions that you need to be aware of:

1. You have a duty of "good faith bargaining" (as required by law). Thus, you can't lie, cheat, or refuse to negotiate with the other party.

2. The company has been and most likely will remain unionized for quite some time. Therefore, it is important for both parties, not only to reach an agreement that will satisfy their constituents, but also to maintain some type of relationship with the other party.

Background information: The company, the Marion Monitor Manufacturing Company (MMM), produces monitors for computers of all sizes, shapes, and models. The company was highly profitable in the 1980s; however, due to increased competition, both foreign and domestic, the company's profits have steadily decreased. Nonetheless, the company is still making a rather hefty profit each year. The company fears that if it doesn't "tighten its belt," the company could be in serious financial trouble in a few years. The company would like to regain its status as the leader in monitor manufacturing. The union, the United Monitor Workers (UMW), would like very much to see the workers at MMM compensated comparable to other members of UMW. The union feels that MMM does not share the profits adequately with their employees and thus MMM employees are paid well below other unionized monitor manufacturing employees. Below are the revenues and expenses for the company for the last five years:

Year	Revenues	Expenses
1991	$29.7 million	$21.1 million
1992	$33.1 million	$25.2 million
1993	$36.6 million	$29.0 million
1994	$37.8 million	$31.6 million
1995	$40.0 million	$34.9 million

Management Side

Issue #1: **Wages**: *Current average wage at MMM: $10.35/hour*
    Average wage of local nonunionized workers in this industry: $10.25/hour
    Average wage of local unionized workers in this industry: $10.55/hour
    Average wage of unionized workers nationally in this industry: $10.95/hour
    Inflation has increased 5% over the past year.
    Every $.05/hour increase in wages will cost the company $50,000 per year.

Issue #2: **Medical benefits**: *Current agreement: Employees pay the first $250 of medical expenses per year, after $250 is spent the company pays 80% of the remaining medical bills.*
    Typical agreement for nonunionized workers: same
    Typical agreement for local unionized workers: a $150 deductible
    Typical agreement for unionized workers nationally: a $50 deductible
    For every $50 reduction in the deductible will cost the company $20,000 per year

Issue #3: **Holidays & Sick days**: *Current agreement: Employees have 7 paid holidays off and receive 5 sick days per year.*
    Typical agreement for nonunionized workers: 5 paid holidays & 5 sick days
    Typical agreement for local unionized workers: 6 paid holidays & 5 sick days
    Typical agreement for unionized workers nationally: 6 paid holidays & 5 sick days
    Every additional day off will cost the company $25,000 per year

Issue #4: **Retirement fund**: *Current agreement: Employer contributes an additional 3% of an employee's income into an investment account (stocks & bonds).*
    Typical agreement for nonunionized workers: 2%
    Typical agreement for local unionized workers: 4%
    Typical agreement for unionized workers nationally: 5%
    Each additional 1% contribution will cost the company $75,000 per year

Agreement:

    Issue #1: wages   _____

    Issue #2: medical   _____

    Issue #3: time off   _____

    Issue #4: retirement   _____

    TOTAL Cost (or Savings) to Employer: _____

Issue #1: Wages: *Current average wage at MMM: $10.35/hour*
   Average wage of local nonunionized workers in this industry: $10.25/hour
   Average wage of local unionized workers in this industry: $10.55/hour
   Average wage of unionized workers nationally in this industry: $10.95/hour
   Inflation has increased 5% over the past year.
   Every $.05/hour increase in wages will cost the company $50,000 per year.

Issue #2: Medical benefits: *Current agreement: Employees pay the first $250 of medical expenses per year, after $250 is spent the company pays 80% of the remaining medical bills.*
   Typical agreement for nonunionized workers: same
   Typical agreement for local unionized workers: a $150 deductible
   Typical agreement for unionized workers nationally: a $50 deductible
   For every $50 reduction in the deductible will cost the company $20,000 per year

Issue #3: Holidays & Sick days: *Current agreement: Employees have 7 paid holidays off and receive 5 sick days per year.*
   Typical agreement for nonunionized workers: 5 paid holidays & 5 sick days
   Typical agreement for local unionized workers: 6 paid holidays & 5 sick days
   Typical agreement for unionized workers nationally: 6 paid holidays & 5 sick days
   Every additional day off will cost the company $25,000 per year

Issue #4: Retirement fund: *Current agreement: Employer contributes an additional 3% of an employee's income into an investment account (stocks & bonds).*
   Typical agreement for nonunionized workers: 2%
   Typical agreement for local unionized workers: 4%
   Typical agreement for unionized workers nationally: 5%
   Each additional 1% contribution will cost the company $75,000 per year

Agreement:

   Issue #1: wages   _____

   Issue #2: medical   _____

   Issue #3: time off   _____

   Issue #4: retirement   _____

   TOTAL Cash Benefit (or Cost) to Employees: _____

Questions: *Please answer the following questions after the negotiations are finished.*

1. What external factors played the biggest role in the negotiations?

2. How would you describe your negotiations? integrative or distributive?

3. How do you think this style of negotiating will affect future negotiations?

4. How do you think your constituents will react to the agreement you reached?

5. Has your opinion of union/management negotiations changed as a result of this exercise? How?

Exercise 14-2: Clear Contract?

In the previous exercise you negotiated over four issues that often play a key role in collective bargaining. There are other issues that are very important to both union and management that deal with employee discipline. As the chapter points out, in the section titled "Disputes Over Contract Interpretation," grievance arbitration is another critical issue in union/management relations. Listed below are two issues often specified in a union/management contract. A problem occurs in the interpretation of each of them.

Issue #1: Excessive Absenteeism

Policy in the labor contract: *Any employee who is late three times within a three-month period will be suspended for one day without pay. The second time this occurs in a three-month period the employee is suspended for one week. The third time it occurs, the employee will be terminated.*

Situation: Juanita Romerez has shown up late for work three consecutive days in a row. Her supervisor wants to suspend her for one day as specified in the contract. Juanita has contacted the union steward to represent her to contest this penalty. She knows that she has been late three times in a row. However, all three times she has been late by only 5 minutes. Further, Juanita takes the bus to work each day. She takes the first bus the city runs (6:45 a.m.), but the bus doesn't get her to the company until 7:03 a.m. Thus, by the time she punches in she is 5 minutes late. She cannot afford any other way to get to work. Moreover, she feels the policy is unfair because other employees can show up an hour or more late without any penalty unless it happens three times within a three-month period. Upon further investigation, the company has found that many other employees (predominately minority employees) who start work at 7 a.m. and take the bus to work have also been 5 minutes late consistently. Juanita's supervisor was the first to enforce this policy.

Issue #2: Layoff Policy

Policy in the labor contract: *If a layoff is necessary, management agrees to lay off employees in order of seniority regardless of job performance. Those with the most seniority are the last to be laid off.*

Situation: The company, with union approval, has decided to reduce its labor force across the board by 10% due to reduced consumer demand. The company has gone through its employee roster by job category and has discovered a major problem. There are employees in job categories with less organizational tenure than other employees in that category, but have greater job tenure than other employees. Further, there are employees in different departments with differing levels of tenure.

For example, Larry Logan is a crew chief in the plastics division. He was promoted to crew chief 3 years ago. He has been with the company for 25 years. Jerry Johnson is also a crew chief in the plastics division. However, he was hired in this position 15 years ago. Thus, he has greater job tenure than Larry (15 compared to 3), but less organizational tenure than Larry (15 compared to 25). Who should be let go first in accordance with the policy? Further, Harry Houseman is a crew chief in the rubber division. He has been with the company 7 years, four of which as crew chief. Should Harry be let go before Larry or Jerry even though he is in a different division? There are also plenty of entry-level laborers (positions below crew chief on the organizational chart). Should these employees be factored into the layoff of crew chiefs? Whoever the company chooses to lay off will most likely contact the union steward to prevent the job loss.

Questions:

1. If you were the arbitrator, how would you resolve each issue? Why?

    Issue #1: Excessive Absenteeism

    Issue #2: Layoff

2. At first glance both policies seem quite clear. From the situations described, however, you can see both issues need to be substantially revised. How would you revise them?

Issue #1: Excessive Absenteeism

Issue #2: Layoff

Name: _____   Date Due: _____

Exercise 14-3: Unionization & I/O Psychology: Stimulus Response

You are an I/O psychologist working as an independent consultant. You have been recently contacted by the CEO of a midsize manufacturing firm located in a large metropolitan area. You meet with the CEO later that day to find out he is very concerned about his company becoming unionized. When he pulled into the executive parking lot today, he noticed several employees congregating in the employee lot before work. He sent his assistant out into the employee lot to find out what was going on. The assistant came back with a flyer from a local union that he found on the ground. This union has organized several of the company's competitors in the area and nationwide. The assistant wasn't able to find any employee willing to talk to him to find out what spurred this interest in unionization. All employees denied that they were discussing the formation of a union. The CEO would like your help to prevent the formation of a union in his organization.

1. What information would you want to find out about this company?

2. What information would you want to find out about unionized companies in this industry?

3. What information would you want to find out about this particular union?

4. What are the steps for the formation of a union?

5. What legal activities can management undertake to persuade employees not to unionize?

6. What management activities would be illegal in trying to prevent unionization?

7. What areas of I/O psychology will be affected the most if the company becomes unionized? Explain.

ERGONOMICS AND WORK CONDITIONS

The following is a list of key terms and concepts as they are presented in Chapter 15. As a way to help you understand this chapter, go through each of the terms and describe them fully. Then compare your responses to the responses in the text.

Ergonomics:

a) gero-ergonomics:

Ergonomic approaches to work design:

a) Anthropometric approach:

b) Biomechanical approach:

c) Physiological approach:

d) Overview:

Human/Computer interactions in the workplace:

a) computer-aided monitoring:

Safety and accidents:

Safety legislation:

a) OSHA:

Psychological approaches to accident reduction:

a) Personnel selection approach:

b) Ergonomic approach:

c) Personnel training approach:

d) Overview:

Physical stressors in the workplace:

a) Noise:

1) frequency:

2) intensity:

3) the effects of noise:

4) hearing loss from work:

b) Heat:

1) air temperature:

2) humidity:

3) air flow:

c) Cold:

d) Multiple stressors:

Fatigue:

a) Muscular:

b) Mental:

c) Emotional:

d) Skills:

Work schedules:

a) Shift work:

b) Flextime:

c) Compressed workweek:

d) Telecommuting:

Alcoholism and drug abuse in the workplace:

a) Effects on work behavior:

b) Drug testing:

c) Employee Assistance Programs:

Web Sites for Chapter 15

1) http://www.telecommute.org/

This is the web site for the International Telework Association and Council.

2) http://www.gilgordon.com/

This is another web site devoted to telecommuting.

3) http://www.osha.gov/

This is OSHA's web site.

4) http://www.osha-slc.gov/SLTC/ergonomics/

This is OSHA's web site devoted to ergonomics.

5) http://stats.bls.gov/oshhome.htm

This web site provides statistics on safety and health from the Bureau of Labor Statistics.

6) http://www.efr.org/mgmt1.html

This web site is an example of an employee assistance program.

Name: _____   Date Due: _____

Exercise 15-1: Changing the Lock to Fit the Key

One of the key issues in this chapter is that there are three ergonomic approaches to work design: anthropometric, biomechanical, and physiological. The intent of this exercise is to help you better understand these approaches by applying them to a job you are familiar with. Your instructor may have you complete this assignment individually or in groups.

Step #1: Select a job. (The job you choose should be one your classmates can relate to.)

Job title: _____

Step #2: Anthropometric approach. As you know, anthropometry is the study of people in terms of their physical dimensions (e.g., size of one's body, distance between one's elbow and fingertips). The use of this information is necessary in designing ergonomic work equipment or materials (e.g., height of a desk chair).

Describe **two** physical dimensions of employees in the selected job and how the work environment should be designed in order to be ergonomically compatible.

Physical dimension #1: _____

Work environment:

Physical dimension #2: _____

    Work environment:

Step #3: Biomechanical approach. As you know, biomechanics is the application of mechanical principles to the analysis of body-part structure and movement. This approach is concerned with designing tasks or training employees to perform tasks in a way that minimizes the stress, pain or fatigue on human muscles, tendons, and nerves.

Based upon the selected job, identify **two tasks** that involve human movement that could result in stress, pain, or fatigue in employees (either immediately or over time). Then offer a solution for each task to minimize this stress, pain, or fatigue.

    Task #1: _____

    Effect on employee:

Solution:

Task #2: _____

Effect on employee:

Solution:

Step #4: Physiological approach. As you know, the physiological approach to work design examines the impact of task (or job) performance on circulation, respiration, and metabolism. The goal here is to design work within the limits of oxygen flow, blood flow, heart rate, and blood pressure. We don't want employees to experience fatigue on the job, which could result in errors and accidents.

Based upon the selected job, identify **two aspects** of the job that you could relate to some physiological outcomes (e.g., heart rate). Once again, please offer a suggestion to reduce or minimize the physiological impact of the tasks.

Task #1: _____

Physiological effect:

Solution:

Task #2: _____

Physiological effect:

Solution:

Step #5: Which of the three approaches would be the most helpful to redesign your job to be more ergonomic? Explain.

Exercise 15-2: Break a Leg

You work in a private consulting firm as an industrial/organizational psychologist. Your latest client is Bud Billing's Construction (BBC). BBC builds residential properties, typically two-story homes. The company is having problems with on-the-job accidents. The accident rate at BBC is twice the industry average. You have spent the last few days trying to uncover the cause(s) of the high accident rate. Based upon reviewing records and interviewing BBC employees you have come to the following conclusions:

1. There are certain employees at BBC who are involved in accidents much more often than other employees. These "high accident rate employees" are in a variety of jobs. The injuries they sustain also fall in a wide variety of categories (e.g., broken legs, cuts, dislocated shoulders). Fellow employees describe them as: unpredictable, aggressive, unhappy, and risk taking.

2. There are certain jobs at BBC that have higher accident rates than others. Furthermore, these jobs have a tendency to produce one particular type of injury. For example, the job of a framer (incumbent using a nail gun constructs the frame of the house) has a high number of shoulder injuries. The gofers (they pick up and bring wood to the framers) have a high number of back injuries.

3. The most common complaint of BBC employees is that they have never been told or shown safe and unsafe ways of doing their job. BBC does hire highly competent workers. These employees know how to do their jobs, but have virtually no exposure to safety rules, regulations or procedures.

Based upon the above information, answer the following questions.

1) What do you think are the financial consequences of the high accident rate at BBC?

2) What areas of I/O psychology do you see as contributing to the accidents at BBC?

3) What solution(s) would you recommend to BBC to reduce the prevalence of accidents?

Exercise 15-3: I'm Exhausted

Another important section of this chapter deals with the four main types of fatigue: muscular, mental, emotional, and skills. This exercise is designed to help you differentiate among these four terms by first having you match the appropriate type of fatigue with certain jobs. Then, based upon which type of fatigue you think applies to each job, you need to offer a possible intervention to reduce or minimize the effect of this fatigue.

Step #1: Matching. *Match the type of fatigue you feel is most appropriate for each job. Keep in mind you must use each type **at least twice** and you **cannot use one type of fatigue more than three times**. Certain jobs may have more than one type of fatigue that could be applicable. Be prepared to defend your responses.*

<u>JOBS</u>   <u>TYPES OF FATIGUE</u>

___ 1. Chemist   A) Muscular

___ 2. Kindergarten teacher   B) Mental

___ 3. Data entry clerk   C) Emotional

___ 4. New York City cab driver   D) Skills

___ 5. Marriage counselor

___ 6. Brick layer

___ 7. Word processor/Typist

___ 8. Surgeon

___ 9. Suicide hotline staff member

___ 10. Grocery check-out clerk

Step #2: Intervention. *For each type of fatigue, select a job that corresponds to this type of fatigue (based upon your above responses) and come up with some type of intervention that could help eliminate or reduce fatigue on this job.*

1. **Muscular: job** ⟶ _____

    Intervention:

2. **Mental: job** ⟶ _____

    Intervention:

3. Emotional: job $\longrightarrow$ _____

    Intervention:

4. Skills: job $\longrightarrow$ _____

    Intervention: